THE COVENANT OF LOVE

The Covenant of Love

by Janina Babris

Prow

1600 W. Park Avenue
Libertyville, IL 60048

Ecclesiastical Approbation

ISBN 0-913382-19-1

Contents

Illustrations

Maps

Foreword

THE COVENANT OF LOVE is the story about Biblical people in the Old Testament and is written, like the Bible itself, for everyone. In the Bible man is shown with all his weaknesses, shortcomings and dependence on God. God alone is holy and perfect. Man, as long as he depends on God, can attain great things, as Joshua did during the battle with the Philistines: God stopped the course of the sun and moon until the battle was won.

In writing this story many descriptive details were used in order to make the book easily read and enjoyed. These elaborations, personal and relevant to the human scene at all times of man's history, are not unfaithful to the spirit of the scriptural account.

The Bible shows that all men are sinful — even God's especially chosen ones, such as Kings David and Solomon. God created man in his likeness and made a covenant with him. This covenant of love is salvific grace enduring through all ages. God implanted the notion of this covenant in Adam's mind at the most tragic and hopeless moment in Paradise, right after the disobedience to God's will, when Adam and Eve were hiding from the sight of their Creator. God offered a covenant to Noah and sealed it with the rainbow in the sky. God made a more binding covenant with Abraham, and later with Moses, with the Ten Commandments. Then he established a "Father-son" relationship with David, promising him an everlasting throne.

In creating man, God gave him free will. As a father he loved his creation — man: undependable, changeable and unstable . . . "whose heart and mind incline to evil." Throughout the ages he leads man closer to himself step by step, revealing himself by subtle ways.

In writing this story of God's love for mankind, the attempt was made to show that God has been the loving Father from the beginning to the end. Many and various sources were used to accomplish this work; however, the main source was the Old Testament. Most quotations are taken from the Revised Standard Version, Catholic Edition.

It is hoped that this work will inspire the reader to open the Bible — the unending source of revelation — and find the ever-living characters there. No attempt has been made to show the research, although much has been done in order to make the book easily read and enjoyed.

Acknowledgment and gratitude go to Ann Flynn for editing the manuscript with deep insight, to the artist Albert Vasils for original illustrations and to all and everyone who helped to make this work come into existence.

Preface

Janina Babris is a storyteller This is important in today's world of instant and exciting communications when so many people find reading a burden instead of a pleasure. But well-told stories are always a pleasure, and this is especially true of *The Covenant of Love.*

As its title indicates, Mrs. Babris' book is a story about the Chosen People of the Old Testament. Israel's periods of belief and disbelief, God's anger, Israel's repentance, God's forgiveness all come vibrantly alive in modern, spritely language that entertains, educates and enthralls the reader, whether he be adult, or adolescent.

But Janina Babris is also a teacher who carefully weaves her story point-by-point, generation by generation. She systematically presents the people, the stories and the truths found in the Old Testament along with its rich insights into human psychology and fascinating descriptions of historical persons, places and cultures.

For those readers who want to learn *Bible* history, this book lends itself well to outlining and to the construction of time lines — devices which can be of tremendous help to the casual and serious student alike. But even though it is as detailed as a text book, "Covenant" is as enjoyable as an historical novel. Essentially it is the story of God's people — the Chosen and un-Chosen alike. From creation to the time of Christ, it reads like a family history covering many generations — a type of book that has grown quite popular among U.S. readers of late.

Mrs. Babris uses language skillfully with great effect. For instance, the "Voice of Eden" is both a synonym for God and an evocative device that allows us, the readers, to conjure up our own image of the Lord — not her image, nor the image our teachers and parents may have given us. In this way she strengthens the readers' commitment to the story, bonding traditional, often-told accounts with refreshing, imaginative insights.

Terms, names, developments, concepts, and biblical excerpts that are not easily grasped by readers of any age are also defined and explained within the context of the story. In addition, the author also ties recent archeological findings in with the biblical events.

The Covenant of Love is a story through which the Bible itself becomes less formidable, more appealing, and more familiar. It presents to us the rich religious symbolism, prophecy and theology that developed during Old Testament times, and relates them both to the New Testament and to Catholic life today. As story follows story, the reader becomes aware that each is heading towards an expected event: the birth of the Messiah, Christ. In the process, lessons about human nature in general and about our current society in particular are offered in an up-to-date and thoroughly interesting way.

The unusual woodcuts of Albert Vasils used to interpret the story contribute a feeling of irrepressible life and movement to the book. Like the storytelling art of the author herself, Vasil's provocative images will stimulate the reader's own imagination to fill out and complete the picture, and thus immerse him or her yet more in the story.

I recommend *The Covenant of Love* both to those who already know the Scriptures, and to those — especially young people — who have not yet discovered the fascinating treasures of the Bible. Mrs. Babris is an enthusiastic, fascinating guide. The proof of her competence and her art will be the reader's growing desire and readiness to go back to the Old Testament and read the actual biblical text itself. This, I think, is the greatest value of her book.

REV. BERNARD M. GEIGER, O.F.M.CONV.

March 14, 1979

Chapter I

The Story of Creation

1. The Beginning of Rotation

How did the world begin? Has this question revolved in your mind as many times as it has in mine? *Revolved.* Yes, that is it! The whole world — the universe — revolves, rotates, spins and whirls. That must be the beginning.

Genesis, the first Book of the Holy Bible, contains a beautiful story about it: "In the beginning God created the heavens and the earth."

What is heaven? Is it an open space, a great expanse, the atmosphere, harmony and order? Or, is it all this and much more? Heaven was "created," so it must be something that exists, a place.

"And the earth was without form and void, and darkness was over the face of the deep. The Spirit of God hovered over the water."

The entire universe was formless until the Spirit of God moved it, until God put everything into motion, into rotation. Rotation was the very first movement, the cause of things taking on shape, form.

The universe became an immense merry-go-round that continuously revolves, and, through this rotation, forms new clusters of rotating, energized objects.

And God said, 'Let there be light,' and there was light. And God saw that the light was good and he divided the light from the darkness.

For God to create anything, he needs merely to wish it, to say a word; if, for even one second, he withdrew this wish there would be nothing. The whole universe exists in God and depends on him.

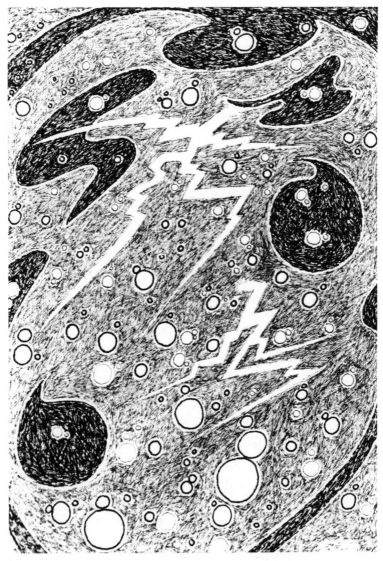

The spirit of God hovered over the water.

God is Existence, Living Being. Only a being can delight in something. God saw light and was delighted. He said, "It is good!" He liked it!

"He called the light 'day' and the darkness 'night.' Evening and morning came: the first day."

Now everything was rotating according to God's will.

> *And God said, 'Let there be a firmament to separate water from water.' God called the firmament 'heaven.' Evening and morning came: the second day.*

The Book of Genesis goes on to tell us how God gathered the waters together into a single mass and called them "seas." The dry land he called earth." "And God saw it was good." As a painter, when his drawing is sketched, starts to put color into his picture, so God colored the earth giving it green grass, a variety of flowers, trees, shrubs and herbs, telling them to grow and bear fruit, each with seed according to its kind. "And it was so. God saw it and knew it was good! Evening and morning came: the third day."

> *God created lights in the firmament of heaven, a light for the day and lights for the night. These are the signs for the seasons, days and years. And there came evening and morning: a fourth day.*

2. The Creation of Living Beings

When everything was firmly set and revolving, each on its own axis and traveling in its own path around the others in perfect order and precision, when the earth was yielding an abundance of fruit, God told living creatures to abound in the waters and winged creatures to fly above the earth.

> *And God blessed them, saying, 'Be fruitful,*
> *and multiply, and fill the waters of the seas, and let*
> *birds multiply on the earth.'*

That was the fifth day of creation and God was delighted for "He saw that it was good."

In following the text of Genesis we read that God told the earth to produce vegetation, to bring out all kinds of living creatures. Everything in water and on earth was created this way. The water and earth were begetting and bearing the plants and the creatures, everything that grows and moves according to God's wish, "Let there be!"

> *On the sixth day of creation God said, 'Let*
> *the earth bring forth the living creatures after their*
> *kind, and everything that creeps upon the earth*
> *after his kind: and it was so.*

Still referring to the sixth day, the Book of Genesis suddenly changes when it describes the creation of man. God is now addressed in the first person instead of "he" and God speaks in the plural, using "Us."

> *'Let us make man in our image, after our like-*
> *ness: and let them be masters of the fish of the sea,*
> *of the fowl of the air, of all living animals of the*
> *earth, and of all the earth.' God saw all he had*
> *made, and indeed it was very good. Evening and*
> *morning came: the sixth day.*

It seems like God took a very personal interest in creating his new creature — man. He would be a creature superior to all others, and even much more, one who would reflect the likeness of God himself.

God set to work like a great sculptor, He, the First Sculptor, created not merely shapes and images, but entirely new beings, having life in themselves. He took the dust of the earth, mixed it with water and it became a pliable clay. From it he shaped a new

Joy and gratitude welled up in Adam's chest.

molding tall and slender. But clay in itself has no life. The new
form lay on the ground just like any statue carved by a master in
later ages. God leaned over the new creature and breathed into
its nostrils the breath of life. The creation came to life, becoming
body and soul—a man!

3. The Beginning of Mankind's History

In the shade of a tree the newly-formed man slept. It was
early morning, the first dawn of his life. The stir of birds in the
branches above made him aware of himself. His eyes were still
closed, but he knew he was breathing. He felt his heart beating and
warm blood streaming through his veins, circulating to the tips of
his toes from his heart and back again throughout the tissues of
his living body.

He slightly moved his arms, his legs, just to feel them. With
this motion he was suddenly awake, fully conscious. He raised his
eyelids.

As he opened his eyes he was looking, full of wonder and
awe, directly into the face of his Maker. Adam saw in the face
of God a great delight that said to him, "It is good!"

Joy and gratitude—his first emotions—welled up in Adam's
chest as he looked at God's smiling face. He stood up tall and
handsome in the presence of his Lord. He looked at the beauty
surrounding him and, in complete astonishment and awe, made his
first sound of approval, "Ah!"

God's reassuring delight flowed into him. Full of self-confidence, Adam planted his feet firmly on the ground. He knew it was
good to be alive. This earth, full of wondrous surprises, was given
him to explore and discover.

The Lord God showed Adam the Garden of Eden, its flowing
rivers on the banks of which Adam was to live. Then the Lord
took him to the middle of the garden and warned,

From every tree in the garden you may eat.
But you must not eat from the tree of knowledge

*of good and evil, for the day you eat of it you shall
most surely die.*

The test did not seem to be a difficult one. There was such an abundance of fruit in the garden that Adam felt no need to eat from the forbidden tree.

Daily Adam strolled through the Garden of Eden, discovering and naming the plants and animals he met on his way. And the Lord God often walked with him. As Adam walked he sang a song of joy, imitating birds and always uttering new sounds expressing his feelings about the wonderful world.

He was the image of God, closely united to his creator. He was meant to possess and enjoy the earth and all created things. Having received them from God, he gave thanks to him for them.

Since Adam was created with a free will for choosing between good and evil, all that God asked him was obedience: not to eat the fruit from the tree of knowledge. In the beginning it did not preoccupy Adam's thoughts. His days went smoothly and evenly. He often stood under the branches of one tree or another, lost in gratitude and wonder. Then he would raise his hands high and praise the Lord with songs of thanksgiving and glory.

As time passed, Adam's singing took on a different mood. Tunes he sang now seemed longer, his voice ranged high and low, and his stretched out melody searched for an echo. He was taking deep breaths and making new melodies which gradually became songs of joy. He strolled alone among the trees and shrubbery searching for something in the distance, not knowing himself for what.

One evening Adam was lying awake on the ground for a long time. He was thinking. There was some feeling in him that he could not name. With both hands under his head, he lay on his back with eyes wide-open gazing into the starry sky. He felt restless and wondered why he could not fall asleep.

With great compassion, God watched Adam and said to himself, "It is not good that man is alone." The Lord God knew that the time was at hand to give Adam a companion. So he fanned a cooling breeze on Adam putting him into a deep sleep. God then performed the first surgery. He slit open Adam's side and took out one of his ribs, afterwards closing the gap with flesh.

From the clay of the earth God formed another being to Adam's likeness. He put Adam's rib in it and gave her life. She looked like Adam and, yet, was different.

God, holding the new creature's hand, brought her to Adam who was still sleeping. When God looked at Adam he woke up instantly. Upon opening his eyes and seeing a new being like himself, Adam sprang to his feet in amazement. They both stood looking at each other, first with astonishment then admiration and approval. He was tall and muscular with short bushy hair. His dark brown eyes were full of innocence. In the first rays of the morning sun, Adam's smooth skin took on a warm blush.

Adam saw her to be smaller, gentle and beautiful with long golden hair falling softly over her shoulders. Her eyes were greenish-blue like the leaves from the very middle of the garden. He was attracted by her softness and fragileness. Looking at each other, their eyes bounced with joy and their faces gleamed in happiness.

God, watching them, shared their joy. Out of love he had created them and now he delighted in his own work. God's love embraced them. Still looking at each other the first man and his companion joined hands. The Lord God blessed their union, the first marriage. As he blessed them, God's love streamed into their hearts and all three shared mutual affection and joy.

Adam said,

> *She is bone of my bone and flesh of my flesh!*
> *She shall be called woman, for she was taken from*
> *man.*

At the same time Adam set down law,

> *This is why a man leaves his father and moth-*

Although naked, they were not aware of it.

er and joins himself to his wife, and they become
one body.

Adam, made by the hand of God, was a perfect man and she, a perfect woman. They lived in Eden blissfully happy. There was complete harmony between them, and they always revealed their thoughts to one another. Their love for each other increased. They were two unspeakably noble and beautiful persons made for one another, reflecting God's majesty.

Fear, except their holy fear of God, was not known to them. Nature was delicately balanced — animals were friendly and the nature was not inclement, providing the lush greens of the flowers and an abundance of vegetation. There was nothing to fear since man and all elements coexisted in utter harmony.

Adam admired his companion's beauty and gentleness and she loved Adam, his strength and kindness. The air was warm and pleasant in Eden, so their bodies did not need protection. Although naked, they were not aware of it and felt no shame.

In the very middle of the Garden of Eden there stood the tree of life, as well as the tree of knowledge of good and evil. The tree of knowledge was thriving, growing faster and more vigorously than any other tree. A thick bark covered its sturdy trunk. Its branches were like a giant's outstretched arms, and their wide dark green leaves were very inviting for a comfortable shade during the early afternoon hours.

Many times Adam passed this particular tree and regarded it with curiosity. He never stopped at it, just slowed down his pace in order to get a better look at it. Sometimes he even walked around it, but his holy fear of God told him to leave the place, so he did. He told his wife all he knew about the tree of knowledge, explaining to her very carefully what God had told him about it. And she promised never to touch it, since death seemed to be a terrible consequence.

One day the woman was strolling alone in the garden. She felt thirsty and thought a drink from the nearby stream would be refreshing. As she turned toward the river she heard a rustle in the shrubbery. Looking in that direction among the leaves and blossoms, she saw a face with two glowing eyes black like coal. It was a serpent.

From the grinning mouth of the newcomer came cunning words, "Is it true that you can't eat fruit from any of the trees in the garden?"

The woman looked puzzled then answered the serpent with open frankness, "Of course not! We may eat the fruit of all the trees except that from the tree of knowledge in the middle of the garden. God said, 'You must not eat it, nor touch it, under pain of death.'"

The serpent laughed. His slim colorful body moved in a long spiral forming circles and loops, twirling around the woman and leaping ahead of her. She was fascinated by this display and followed him toward the center of the garden attracted by the magnetism of his coal black eyes and coiling body.

There in the very middle of Eden the serpent entwined himself around the largest tree, the tree of knowledge of good and evil, saying, "Look, I am on its branches! You shall not die if you touch it. And God knows that when you eat the fruit, your eyes will be opened and you will be like God, knowing good and evil."

The woman looked at the tree. She feared it and at the same time was drawn by curiosity toward it. Her thirst still hadn't been quenched and there, on a branch among thick leaves, dangled a most desirable piece of fruit, ripe and seemingly juicy. Her eyes were caught by its ruddy glow in the sinking sun. The serpent put his weight on the branch from which the fruit hung and bent it lower, putting the fruit just in reach of her hand. Still she hesitated.

"You will have the knowledge," the serpent repeated very politely, still with a mysterious grin on his face.

Knowledge. She knew she wanted knowledge. Maybe just merely to touch it and smell it would do no harm? She clasped her fingers around the fruit and slightly twisted it. The ripened fruit came off with ease. Feeling its cool softness, she lifted it to her face. The fruit had a bittersweet aroma. She bit into it.

As soon as she did, she was frightened. The flavor was nothing at all like anything she had ever tasted. Its sugary sweetness was bewildering, its bitterness brought tears to her eyes, but she chewed the pulp and swallowed it. She even bit off another piece. At this moment Adam approached her and was greatly shocked when he realized what his wife had done.

"Woman!" he called reproachfully. She stood staring at him, her eyes filled with tears. Fear overcame Adam. This woman, given to him, had eaten from the tree of knowledge! Would she now be more knowing and wiser than he? Or maybe even superior? Now since she knew good and evil she could very well be!

With misty eyes full of new dark shades in them that were unknown to Adam, she looked strangely beautiful. He loved the woman and wanted to be like her, wise and knowing. She raised her hand with the half-eaten fruit in it. Its juice trickled between her fingers, running down her arm to her elbow. She slightly extended her hand toward Adam, offering him the fruit. He took it. Looking dazedly into her eyes, he ate the forbidden fruit. They both felt intoxicated from its taste.

Their decision to disobey God's command brought about a great change in them. Their radiance suddenly diminished. The sun at this moment went down. The serpent slithered down the tree and glided away with great haste. Upon acceptance of the forbidden fruit man and woman became instruments of evil. They stood apart from God by their own free will. Upon eating it, man turned away from his Creator, separated from him, becoming a self-willed and self-centered being.

As the serpent foretold, their eyes were opened. They kept looking at each other and suddenly for the first time they realized they were naked. A feeling of shame and guilt gripped them and they hid from each other in the shrubbery. There they gathered some broad leaves from the trees and twined them around their hips as coverings.

In the Garden of Eden at the cool of the day Adam and Eve usually took long walks together with the Lord God. This was the most gratifying part of their day. The direct presence of God was their most elating happiness. That day when evening came they heard God walking in the garden. Adam and his wife were in hiding, afraid to come out. They were distressed and ashamed of themselves.

"Adam!" called the Lord, "Where are you?" No answer. The Lord God called again. "Where are you, Adam?"

Adam hesitated, but when he heard God calling him for the third time he responded, "I heard your voice in the garden. I was afraid because I am naked, and I hid myself."

"Who told you that you are naked?" asked him the Lord. "Have you eaten of the tree of which I commanded you not to eat?"

Adam was sure he had lost the friendship of the Lord God, whom he loved so deeply and who loved him, and before whom he now trembled in fear. Instead of confessing and being repentant about what he had done, he put the blame on the woman.

"The woman you placed at my side," he muttered, "gave me fruit from the tree and I ate it."

What he tried to say was that his fault was not so great after all. The Lord God himself gave this woman to him and she was the one who confused him.

"Why did you do that?" God asked the woman. And she, just like Adam, tried to defend herself by accusing the serpent.

"The serpent beguiled me into eating it," she replied.

"So things stand. The old serpent, the devil, has deceived her," thought the Lord God. And he condemned the serpent for his conquest in paradise. From then on, instead of a beautiful creature, the serpent would be cursed among all the animals. Addressing the serpent, the Lord God said, "You shall crawl on your belly and eat dust every day of your life. I will make you enemies of each other: you and the woman, your offspring and her offspring."

The woman was stunned. Even more puzzling to her, were the Lord God's next word to the serpent, "She shall crush your head and you shall lie in wait for her heel." She did not understand such far off prophecy about the coming Redeemer — that the salvation of mankind would come through a woman, "she," who, because of her perfect obedience, would make up for the first woman's disobedience. She did realize, though, that God was giving them hope for their future.

Then, directing his words to the woman, the Lord God foretold her fate: in fear and in pain she will bear the children and her husband will be her master!

And to Adam, the Lord God said:

> *You shall gain your bread by the sweat of your brow until you return to the ground; for from it you were taken. Dust you are, to dust you shall return.*

Adam then spoke to the woman, "You will be called 'Eve,' the mother of the living."

How did Adam find courage to speak at this moment? Did he feel that she needed his support, because she looked so sad and frail? Did God himself reveal this prophetic truth to Adam? At the moment of condemnation when they knew that death was a consequence of their sin, it would have been more natural for Adam to have said to his wife that she would become the mother of all who would *die*. But quite to the contrary, although he knew they deserved death for their opposition to God's will, Adam named his wife Eve, "Mother of all the living." Apparently God's mercy was revealed to Adam at this very moment, as well as the idea of the forthcoming Redeemer.

After showing them this first glimmer of salvation, the Lord God acted like a Father to his children. He made garments of animal skins and clothed them.

Then God said,

> *See, the man has become like one of us, with his knowledge of good and evil. He must not be allowed to stretch his hand out next and pick from the tree of life also, and eat some and live forever.*

Thus, he led Adam and Eve from the Garden of Eden, and at the entrance to the garden he stationed the cherubim with a flaming sword, to guard the way to the tree of life. With the closing of paradise their eyes became blindfolded to spiritual beings. They could no longer see God as they used to see him, nor the angels.

4. The First Family of Mankind

Life outside of paradise was indeed very different from the life they had led while living in the Garden of Eden. The earth was basically the same but nature had changed. Rain and storms, thunder and lightning threatened Adam and Eve. Sometimes there were long periods of drought, making the land too dry to produce crops. Just as the Lord God had warned, they would have to work hard for food and clothing — unlike before. Shelter was now a necessity because of the weather and because of the wild beasts roaming the land in search of their prey.

More and more Adam and Eve had to depend on each other. Each needed the other to survive. Sometimes they became sad and disheartened and even argued with one another; the harmony between them was lost. But the most painful experience for them was to lose the presence of God which they had constantly felt and cherished while in paradise.

The Holy Bible says: "The man knew Eve and she conceived." Their first union as man and wife gave them new knowledge of each other, enabling them to take part in God's creativity.

One day when Adam returned from the field Eve told him with happy excitement, "I have gotten a man with the help of the Lord!" Eve became the mother of living descendants taking life from God with his sanction and approval.

The first parents rejoiced over the birth of their first child. How proud was Eve to put the first-born son into the arms of Adam! Here, indeed, was proof that God had not forsaken them. This child, as every child born into the world, is the best evidence of God's hope in mankind.

They named him Cain* and, instantly, they loved their help-less infant. Since both Adam and Eve were created as adults, they had to learn how to take care of him.

A year later they had another son and named him Abel. As so often happens, from birth the two boys were entirely different. Cain was husky and a man of action. Abel, shorter in stature, had a more gentle disposition. Cain, even as a young boy, was of quick temper, while Abel was easygoing and soft-spoken. Because of their differences it was easy for Abel to win his parents' affection. Although they loved them both, Eve spent more time with Abel than with Cain. When Cain noticed his mother more often talking and laughing with his brother, it aroused a deep jealousy in him. Wasn't he the older one to whom more respect and attention belonged?

As nomads do even today, the first family moved from place to place in search of better pastures and fields. They settled in one place for a while and when that land did not provide enough to feed the family and their flock, they moved on again. Cain, a man of strength, tilled the soil. Abel was a shepherd, keeper of the flock.

Cain and Abel knew well how their father and mother were created. Adam and Eve told them the whole truth about their creation, life in paradise and their disobedience to God. The same story was repeated many times to both boys until they knew it by heart. They were told about God and how their parents saw him in paradise and talked with him. They knew, too, that when their parents were ousted from the Garden of Eden, God's voice could no longer be heard and his presence no longer seen.

*Hebrew. ganah — get

Cain and Abel wanted to make an offering to God — perhaps to try to make amends or as an apology to him for the sin of their parents. They each decided to build an altar on which to place their sacrifice. One by one they carried small and large stones in from the field and laid them one upon the other.

Cain harvested some fruits from his field and put them on his altar. Abel carried a fat first-born of his flock and likewise placed it on his altar near Cain's. The two brothers lit their offerings. The fat from Abel's sacrifice created an intense flame with smoke billowing straight upward. The flames on Cain's offering were smothered by the smoke which hung close to the ground.

Cain's smoke did not rise at all. He knew the sign. God did not accept his offering. Was it because he kept the best fruit from his field for himself and sacrificed on the altar the ones of lesser quality? Cain wondered what difference it made.

Abel prayed by the altar with his arms lifted upward. He was singing a song of supplication and his voice rose in the same manner as the smoke from his burnt offering. God was noticeably pleased with Abel's sacrifice and soon the song of petition turned to one of thanksgiving and glorious praise.

Cain was enraged and resentful about the favor his brother was shown. God did not have any regard for him! He left his sacrifice muttering angry words, "Is it not enough that my mother prefers this weakling boy? Now even the Lord shows his preference for him!"

The Lord God heard Cain and with His fatherly concern asked him:

> *Why are you sad? If you do well, shall you*
> *not be accepted? If you do not do well, will not sin*
> *crouch at the door? Its desire is for you, but you*
> *must master it!*

Having given the man free will, how much more could God do for him? He warned him with his own voice, showing the angered man the root of his anger and assuring him, "if you do

When Cain saw that life was gone from his brother's body
he realized that what he did was very wrong.

well. . ." you will be accepted. Cain knew this voice and had no doubt as to whom it belonged. He heard enough about this voice from his parents.

Instead of regret and contrition, instead of turning his face to God, Cain became even more enraged. The thought of murder entered his mind. He rejected God's help and decided to take things into his own hands and find a quick solution to it, once and for all!

At sundown Cain said to his brother, "It has been a long time since you have seen the fields that I till. Let us go for a walk, brother, and I will show you the produce of my work."

Abel was glad indeed. Cain spoke to him in a kindly manner so seldom that he joyfully agreed to take a walk with his elder brother.

When they were in the field Cain let Abel walk ahead while he lingered behind. Picking up a heavy rock, Cain threw it at the head of his brother. Abel fell to the ground.

On bended knees Cain lifted his brother's shoulders from the ground. When he saw that life was gone from his body, Cain shook him desperately and called, "Abel! Abel!" as though wanting to awaken him from a deep sleep. But Abel's body was limp and heavy.

This, the first death on earth, occurred as a direct result of sin, as a revolt against the will of God. Cain realized that what he did was very wrong. He was so frightened that all he could think of was escaping, getting away from the scene of the crime. And he started to run. He ran and ran into the darkness of night until he fell down on the ground, breathless and exhausted.

"Where is your brother?" called the Lord.

"I do not know," answered Cain. "Am I my brother's keeper?"

Even today we hear Cain's question asked in many different ways. Sometimes we hear it verbatim and out loud. Most often, though, we "hear" it from silent bystanders who decide not to become involved in their brother's misfortune. Apparently God does want us to be our "brother's keeper," as we learn from his reply to Cain:

> *What have you done? The voice of your*
> *brother's blood cries to me from the ground.*

And the Lord cursed the soil that had received Abel's blood, saying that it would no longer yield any crops for him, no matter how hard he toiled. He condemned Cain to the life of a "fugitive and a wanderer."

Cain's conscience already told him that his sin was a great one. A life spent away from home in the unknown and unfriendly world had to be his fate. Full of fear and terror he pleaded with the Lord.

"My punishment is too great to bear. You are driving me from my land and from you. Whoever finds me will kill me!"

Had he lost everything? The land of his birth, God's protection? Would everyone whom he met be his enemy?

"Not so!" Again God spoke as a Father to his son. "Not so! Whomever kills you will receive seven times your punishment."

Then the Lord gave Cain a sign. He put a mark on him as a warning for others not to kill him.

Cain became the first murderer and fugitive in history. He wandered from place to place, farther and farther away from his parental dwelling. Finally he settled in the land of Nod, east of Eden.

Because he was a marked man he was different from others. He became a man whom others feared. He could no longer till the soil, because since God cursed it, the land had resisted Cain's efforts to produce crops. He had to find a trade other than farming in order to keep himself alive. Cain became a builder.

In the land of Nod, which means "wanderer," he met a woman who fell in love with him and became his wife. Be it the Creator's or a creature's, love from the very beginning has been a mystery. It always makes us wonder. How could this woman love a murderer, a fugitive with a mark on himself, a man who seemingly did not deserve love?

Cain built a few dwellings and in this way founded a city. Possibly it was just a cluster of people living close to each other, working together, sharing and depending on each other's efforts.

Cain's wife gave birth to a son. God had given him the honor of fatherhood, offering him new hope in his son! Proud and happy about his offspring, Cain named the city after his firstborn, Enoch.

God, in his infinite goodness, blessed Cain with many progeny, many quite remarkable people. Some of his descendants were notable musicians who made harps and flutes. From generation to generation they passed down this trade, as well as the fine arts of playing the instruments and singing. Others became metal craftsmen, forerunners of those who would forge exquisite vessels of bronze and iron.

God's grace and mercy was still with them, although his face was withdrawn from them.

5. A Flood of People Destroyed by Deluge

Cain's violence was a frightening shock to his parents, Adam and Eve. For the first time they faced death as a result of their sin of disobedience in paradise. Cain was gone. Their gentle son Abel was buried in the ground. They had lost them both and grieved over their loss.

Many years passed. Adam and Eve lived alone in the shadow of their original sin, always longing for God's presence, never forgetting the bliss of the Garden of Eden. Their sorrow was even more deepened when Adam, after Cain's crime, began to avoid Eve and spent a great deal of time alone in the woods.

The harmony between the first two people was disrupted, their moods became changeable. Adam felt depressed and reproached Eve for listening to the cunnings of the serpent in paradise.

"Look, Adam," protested Eve, "you always walked around the tree of knowledge wondering about it!"

"Yes," lamented Adam, "but if you had not eaten that fruit and had not given it to me, we would still be in the perfect happiness and security of Eden. Now we have lived away from paradise for over a century, awaiting our deaths."

Eve was neither ready nor willing to give in to despair and hopelessness. Although it had been a hundred and thirty years since they left paradise, she had not aged much. She never forgot that Adam named her "mother of the living." She mused that there must be more than this in God's plan. Eve did what women today do when their marriage starts to go flat or become dull. . . .

One evening the first woman prepared a better meal than usual for her husband and carefully adorned herself. Sitting by the fire and enjoying a well-cooked meal, Adam looked at Eve with admiration. It had been a long time since he had noticed her. He saw that she was indeed beautiful and lovable.

From that day on, new joy and hope filled the life of the first family. One morning Eve announced news of gladness to her husband.

"God has blessed us again. We will need a new cradle!"

Adam fathered another son, a son to his own likeness. He named him Seth. Again Eve was the "mother of the living." After Seth, who grew up to be very much like Abel, they had many sons and daughters during the remainder of their nine hundred and thirty years on earth. The many generations which descended from their children were made up of both obedient and disobedient people.

Many centuries passed. The earth was populated by all kinds of people, good and bad. Most turned away from God and walked their own ways. God knew this and cautioned them from time to time. Only a few heeded the Lord's warnings. Instead, the majority became more and more selfish, leading lives full of evil and violence.

Although Cain moved far away into the East, after many generations his descendants multiplied into great numbers and united with Seth's. When the sons of God saw the fair maidens of the sons of men they took them as their wives. Each married as many as he wanted.

From the mixture of these two races, the giants of men were born. Some of these people were renowned and mighty. The combination of two races caused an "explosion" of population. The new generation were very large people with extraordinary long life spans. Most of them lived to be more than nine hundred years old, as did Adam and Eve.

The Lord God saw the danger of overpopulation and felt the wickedness of mankind growing. He said,

My spirit shall not remain in man forever,
since he is flesh. His lifetime shall be no more than
one hundred and twenty years.

God is master of life and death. He gives life and can take it away whenever he pleases. As long as man lives, God's spirit lives within him. When the spirit is withdrawn, man's body turns into the dust of the earth.

The story about the first parents and their Creator was faithfully conveyed from one generation to the next. Only a few lived their lives as though they realized that God is the source of love and goodness who gave them life and was sustaining it in them. Men were falling away from the one true God, worshipping strange gods. They allowed evil to remain in their thoughts and hearts, forgetting God, their Creator.

God, seeing the corruption of man spread, was saddened. The Bible says, "He regretted that he had made man and was grieved to the heart." The cup of God's patience was overflowing fast. He said, "I will wipe from the face of the earth man, my own creation, man and beast."
Noah who tilled the land and did some carpentry work on the side.

Not all men turned away from God. There was a man named

Noah who tilled the land and did some carpentry work on the side. He, a humble and simple-hearted man, walked with God and observed God's laws. When Noah was five hundred years old, he became the father of three sons; Shem, Ham and Japheth. He taught all of his children the virtue of obedience.

One afternoon when he was walking from the field toward his dwelling, a cloud suddenly overshadowed him and he heard a voice. He knew instantly that the Lord God was the one who spoke in this majestic voice. Noah fell on his knees. In front of him was a tall cloud-like column. The Voice coming from the cloud said,

> *I have decided to make an end of all flesh because the earth is filled with violence of man's own making.*

God told Noah that he was going to send a flood to wipe from the face of the earth all men and beasts, as well as the birds of the sky. Water would destroy everything—houses, fields, cities, forests—everything, including all of mankind with the exception of Noah and his sons. They had found mercy in God's eyes and, along with their immediate families, they were spared.

Noah was very sad. Still on his knees, looking up at the towering column which seemed to take on a huge image, he prayed to ward off punishment. Noah begged and pleaded with God to spare mankind, but the Voice answered, "I will destroy them with the earth."

The Lord continued,

> *Make yourself an ark of gopher wood. Make rooms in the ark and cover it inside and out with pitch.*

Such a task was beyond Noah's comprehension. In his humility he asked,

> *How can I build an ark? I am a simple man and more than five hundred years old. I have never seen one nor do I know how to construct such a thing!*

To reassure Noah the Lord gave him a detailed plan — a "blueprint" to follow. The ark had to be three hundred cubits in length and thirty cubits in height. In our present day measure it was to be about four hundred and fifty feet long, seventy-five feet wide and forty-five feet high. "Make it with lower, second and third decks, the Lord continued his instructions.

It was quite a ship which Noah had to build. And, he had never been to sea, had never even seen a large body of water or a seaworthy vessel!

In order to prove his fatherly love for this good man and to strengthen Noah's self-confidence, God made a promise:

> *I will establish my covenant with you. And you shall come into the ark, you, your sons, your wife and your sons' wives with you. And a pair, male and female, of every living thing you must bring into the ark.*

The phrase "to establish a covenant" meant nothing to Noah. The real meaning was hidden from him. Still, he trusted the Lord and, calling his three sons—Shem, Ham and Japheth—set to work.

When God gives a task there is no assurance that it will be an easy one. It does not mean that God will remove all difficulties and obstacles, making it easygoing.

Noah faced one hardship after another. First of all, there were no woods nearby the place where they dwelled and that, of course, meant no lumber. He had to move with his sons and their families to a new place in the mountains. The countryside was covered with hardy, slow-growing gopher trees, probably related to the cedars. It took some time and lots of toil to move all the household. When they were finally settled there, Noah built an altar, piling up the stones. He offered a burnt sacrifice to the Lord when he was finished.

Meantime, the wickedness in mankind kept spreading like wildfire. People prospered and were proud of their "civilization" and progress. They idolized their possessions and worshipped images made of stone and marble. They adored these false gods whom they could manipulate as they saw fit.

The construction of the ark took Noah and his sons a long time. Besides working on it, cutting logs and boards, hauling them on their backs and putting them in place, the four men had to till the fields to provide their families with food and to stock up provisions for the time to be spent on the ark.

Noah's neighbors wondered what he was making. When he explained that he was building an ark and that there would be a great flood through which God would punish the world for its disobedience, they laughed at him. The neighbors ridiculed him and his sons, saying they had all gone mad. Besides insulting them, the people made Noah's work more difficult by stealing his lumber. When Noah told of God's punishment of a deluge they mocked him and called him a "prophet of doom." None heeded his warnings. Instead, they continued to make him the laughing stock of the entire community.

Overcoming all the tribulations and hardships, Noah went on working. God had given him a command and he trusted God, believing he would not be deceived or forsaken.

After the frame of the ark was covered with the rounded roof and the windows were set in place, they worked for many days on the different compartments for animals and grain storage. He partitioned the upper deck with walls for his sons' families. In the middle of the ark was a raised altar, a large wooden table, around which the families would gather for prayer and sacrifice.

When the ark was finished Noah started to cover it with pitch, sealing all the seams inside and outside. When he worked out-of-doors his burden was much greater. Many people, even from great distances, gathered around the ark. It seemed so senseless to build a ship since there was no large body of water within a few hundred miles. They continued to call him a fool and ridiculed him in every way they could think of. Noah endured their malice and mockery, knowing that he was doing the will of God.

After the ark was covered with pitch it shone like a huge black diamond in the midday sun. On the altar near his house, Noah built a fire for sacrifice in thanksgiving to God. All his family gathered around in prayer, singing praises to the Lord.

When all was calm and quiet and the others had gone home to rest, Noah remained at the altar deep in prayer with his hands raised above his head. His face shown in the dim light of glowing coal on the altar. His long white beard reached down to his knees. For his six hundred years of age he looked tall and noble standing erect on the top of the mountain. He was completely absorbed in thanksgiving when he heard the Voice again,

> *I have seen that you are righteous before me in this generation. Go into the ark, you and your household. Bring with you one pair of every living thing to keep them alive with you on the ark.*

Exhausted from the tremendous task of building the ark, Noah replied,

"Lord, I am old! How can I fetch wild beasts, how can I catch the birds in the sky and the creeping things of the ground?"

The Voice answered: "Make yourself a reed. When you play it the animals I have chosen will come to you and you will lead them into the ark. In seven days I will send rain and every living thing that I have created I will blot out from the face of the earth."

Noah once again obeyed God's commands. The nearer the day of chastisement came, the darker grew the sky. Heavy clouds covered the heavens and the sun could no longer be seen. As the roar of thunder became louder and louder and the lightning cut through the clouds near the horizon, people grew frightened. Still, they thought it was merely a severe storm which would pass with the rain. Only Noah realized that the punishment of humanity and the earth was at hand.

He went out in the field and played his reed pipe. The animals, a pair of each kind, came flocking from all the corners of the earth. He led them into the ark. Then the heavens opened up and it started to pour rain.

Noah announced to his family that the prophesied deluge had begun. Gathering his wife, Shem, Ham, Japheth and their wives and children, Noah boarded the ark. The gangplank was pulled in, the doors and windows closed, and "the Lord shut him in."

It continued to rain for forty days. Water inundated the lowlands, causing rivers to swell over their banks, and covered fields, forests and cities. Many tents and houses were afloat in the floodwater. The deluge rose over plateaus and mountain tops. The whole earth was like an endless sea. The ark swelled with the waters, floating wherever the wind blew it.

As the waters rose, anxiety and fear rose in all living things. People saw the ark float away, shining in the bluish light. Some tried to grab hold or get on top of it, but the waves washed them away and they perished. Trees and mountain tops proved to be inadequate refuge from the rising waters. People, realizing their own fate, wept and lamented when they saw their loved ones drown.

The rain kept falling in great torrents, the lightning played in fiery columns. Some people repented for their lives, their turning away from God. But many continued cursing and swearing. Those who repented found mercy and forgiveness in God and saved their souls. Those who despaired, cursing God, were condemned.

Everyone in the closed up ark had a special assignment and had to work hard at the numerous chores. Hundreds of animals and birds had to be fed and their compartments kept clean. Despite what must have been very unpleasant conditions, they all worked in harmony with one another.

The ark sailed atop dark waters in which many dead people, beasts and birds were floating. At last it rested upon a high rocky peak of a mountain chain. The violent rain had stopped. It would be a long time still for the floodwaters to subside and for the earth's surface to return to normal.

Every living thing was blotted from the earth, just as God had foretold.

Only Noah was left and those who were with him in the ark. And the waters prevailed upon the earth a hundred and fifty days.

Noah's faith in God never wavered. He prayed with confidence, and all of his family prayed with him. At last a dry wind blew over the water. Through a small porthole the family in the ark could see the appearance of land!

The sons and grandchildren of Noah kept asking, "Where are we?" But Noah did not know. He had no idea how far away from their home they had sailed. But, was it important? God had provided for them in the past, and they were confident that he would continue to care for them.

Their harbor was the top of Mount Ararat, (Armenia today), about five hundred miles from their original home. It took several years of study by different archeologists and explorers before they agreed that the remnants of a boat found by the farmer named Reskett on Mt. Ararat was Noah's ark.

All of a sudden the legend and "myth" of the Old Testament became a true story. The petrified remains of the boat on the mountaintop surprisingly correspond with the story given in Genesis. The scientists found proof that all of Armenia had once been covered by floodwaters. Not only the Bible, but the mythology of many civilizations tells about a great flood and a certain family who escaped the deluge.

Altogether the ark sailed for seven months before it came to rest. Noah waited another forty days before he opened the porthole of the ark.

He sent out a raven, but it just flew to and fro in an unsuccessful search for food. Then Noah released a dove. Soon the dove returned to the boat so Noah knew that the waters had not yet receded from the earth. After seven more days he sent the dove again. This time it came back with a fresh olive leaf in its beak,

Everyone in a closed up ark had a special assignment and had to work hard on the numerous chores.

and Noah knew that the waters were subsiding from the earth. He waited another week before he removed the ark's covering. He then saw that the ground was dry.

"Go forth from the ark," the Lord God said to Noah. "You, your wife and your sons. . . ."

It took seven days for Noah to unload his ship. But, as soon as the task was completed, he built an altar on the dry ground and praised God for protecting them with such fatherly care. He burned some birds and animals as offerings on the altar. The pleasing fragrance of smoke ascended straight to heaven. When God smelled it he was pleased, saying to Noah that even though "the imagination of man's heart is evil from his youth . . . I will never again curse the ground because of man."

God the Creator explained that his promise to never again destroy the earth was the covenant about which he spoke with Noah before the flood. A rainbow in the sky was to be mankind's reminder of this covenant between God and all living creatures.

The years passed. Noah began farming again, this time adding a grape vineyard to his crops. One day he decided to celebrate their deliverance from destruction in the flood. Noah prepared a sumptuous feast and made wine from the fruit of his vineyard. All of his household joined in the festivities. It was truly a day of jubilee.

Noah was overjoyed. A feeling of safety from all danger and of relief from his great burdens made him very gay. He drank more of the potent wine than his old age could take and he "became drunk and lay uncovered in his tent."

Drunkeness for a patriarch was bad enough, but to lay naked in a tent was a devastating shame. While he was lying like that on the bed, his son Ham entered the tent. He looked at his aged father. It seemed so funny to him that, with a peel of laughter, he called his brothers Shem and Japheth to show them the foolishness of their father. But it did not seem funny to Ham's brothers. Out of respect to their elder, the two brothers entered the tent walking backwards and, without looking at him, covered the nakedness of their father with their capes.

The next day Noah was promptly told what had happened. He never forgot the incident, his shame and embarrassment.

Many summers and winters passed. The descendants of Noah's sons multiplied. The time had come when they had to move on to look for more space, richer fields and greener pastures. Before they parted ways, each in his own direction, Noah called his sons so that he might bless them.

The three sons knelt before their white-bearded father. He began with the youngest, Ham, father of Canaan and ancestor of the Canaanites:

> Cursed be Canaan. A slave of slaves he shall
> be to his brothers.

Enraged with anger and surprise, Ham protested, "What have I done that my descendants deserve such a fate?"

But his aged father continued by blessing Shem:

> Blessed by the Lord my God be Shem: . . .
> let Canaan be his slave!

To Japheth he said:

> May God enlarge Japheth, may he live in the
> tents of Shem; and let Canaan be his slave!

Indeed, Noah had not forgotten the incident of his drunkeness nor Ham's reaction to it. Therefore he cursed the land which not only produced Ham's descendants but whose soil also produced powerful wine causing indecent behavior.

Shem, the oldest, was to be forefather of the "chosen people," the Israelites. The goyim or gentiles were to be the descendants of Japheth. Ham was to become the father of the people who, according to Noah, were to be subject to the descendants of both Shem and Japheth.

After the deluge Noah lived for three hundred and fifty years, to the age of nine hundred and fifty. Noah lived a long, good life.

6. The Tower of All Nations

When Noah and his family entered the ark they did so because they were the chosen ones, hand-picked by God himself. One would think that the descendants of such upright people would be good and obedient to God. But they were far from that. After the flood, the population multiplied very rapidly but, it seems, sinfulness multiplied even faster.

In the fertile valley between the the Tigris and Euphrates Rivers, in the land of Shinar (Syria today), there were living a clever and creative people. They quickly acquired knowledge of the different arts and sciences. They knew how to make bricks and mortar, how to construct sturdy, magnificent buildings. They learned to cut and sculpture stone, creating beautiful statues of men and beasts. These carvings were so life-like that they began to worship them as images of God.

Little by little they completely forgot about the one true God. Besides the idols, they also worshipped the stars and prophesied their own future as well as that of other countries and nations. They believed each man's fate was written in the heavens, that the stars guided and influenced man's life, his fortune and misfortune.

The inhabitants of Shinar became prosperous people and, having such a "good" life, they wanted to live forever, or at least to be remembered and admired by all future generations.

Having built their city, these people decided to erect a tower. It was to be the highest tower ever constructed, reaching well above the clouds. They called it "Ziggurat," which, in the Assyrian language, means high tower. It was to serve as a temple for their idols and was to reach heaven where they imagined the gods to dwell. It was cleverly designed in a pyramidal shape, having many stories and terraces, with pillars and winding stairs so people could climb up and talk to the gods, seeking their favors. At the very top they planned a room—a temple—for their sun god Marduk.

The names of those who contributed to this magnificent building were inscribed with words of praise in the vaults and on the pillars. Everything was done with great skill and careful planning, until . . .

> the Lord came down to see the city and the tower
> which the sons of men had built.

He saw the grandeur of the structure. Even if the Lord did not admire it, at least he acknowledged the human accomplishment. Had it been built in honor of God and not out of human pride and folly, it is most certain that God would have supported their undertaking. But the temple for star-worshippers and idolaters was not in God's plan.

The Lord said,

> Behold, they are one people, and they have all one
> language. This is only the beginning of what they
> will do; and nothing that they propose to do will
> now be impossible for them.

The effect of the fruit from the tree of knowledge was deeply rooted in man's heart and mind, and its seed flourished profusely. With one move or word God could make the tower crumble, but this was not his choice. Instead he chose to confuse their language.

Hundreds of people were working on different levels of the building. Word of mouth was the only means of communication the workers had. They passed orders by calling from one to another. Suddenly the laborer did not understand what the foreman said, the foreman could not understand what his supervisor was shouting to him. Everybody talked, yelled and swore, but not one could understand the other. Orders were shouted into the air and not carried out.

> Therefore its name was called Babel, because the
> Lord confused the language of all the earth,

states the Bible.

It became impossible to go on with the construction of the tower. Confusion and anger were everywhere. The laborers left their places, and the architects left their blueprints. The structure was never finished.

Suddenly the laborer did not understand what his foreman said...

Disappointed and frustrated, everyone left the city. People scattered over the whole earth forming new cities, new tribes, nations and countries — each group speaking a different language. This created a great deal of misunderstanding among them, leading to mutual distrust, violence and war.

Today in the city of Babylon—once noted for its wealth, magnificence and wickedness—one can find only the floor or base of the tower. The first effort to build the tower of all nations was not realized.

Chapter II

The Time of the Patriarchs

7. A Promise and a Trial

From generation to generation, even though people were scattered over the whole earth and spoke different languages, the story of Eden was faithfully recounted when family members gathered around the table or hearth. But the more years that elapsed, the less people were impressed by the lesson it offered. They were leading sinful lives, rejecting the one true God who made them in his own image. They made new gods for themselves, according to their own likeness, and worshipped them.

On the banks of the Euphrates in Ur, home of the Chaldeans, lived Terah with his sons Abram, Nahor and Haran. Haran died as a fairly young man, leaving his small son, Lot. Terah cared for his grandson Lot until just after Abram married Sarai. Since Sarai was childless, she and Abram took Lot into their household.

As was the custom in those days, Terah ruled his family, making decisions for all. He was a descendant of Noah and never failed to remind his sons, telling about the horrors of the deluge. He was proud to belong to the chosen family. This also made him a descendant of Heber from whose name later was derived "Hebrew."

One day Terah decided to leave Ur and the Chaldeans to find richer pastures. From the traders in passing caravans he heard about a fertile valley, the land of Canaan. He made this his destination.

Taking his sons and their wives, his grandchildren and the servants, he headed northwest toward the Mediterranean Sea. When they reached Haran, about 500 miles from Ur, they settled down. Terah was quite old now and exhausted from the long journey. There he died at the age of two hundred and five.

They did not find life any better in Haran than in Ur. People were worshipping idols in the same fashion and their way of life did not follow in the footsteps of God. Here, as well as in Ur, people were greedy, drank excessively, gambled, mistreated their servants and, in general, gave way to their passions.

Abram rejected their lifestyle, as well as their false gods. He refused to take part in human sacrifice as the people of Haran practiced. They riduculed him. Even more, because he believed in one God, the Creator, God of Truth and Justice, his neighbors began to despise him.

God saw Abram's tribulation and rejoiced in his faithfulness. One day while working in the field, Abram heard the Voice,

> Leave your land, your relatives and your clan and
> go to the land which I will show you, and I will
> make of you a great nation.

Being a simple and humble man, Abram obeyed the Voice immediately. He told his wife Sarai to take down the tent. They left in the early dawn of morning, taking with them Lot, the servants and their possessions—all they and their camels could carry. They headed for the land of Canaan. Wasn't that where his father, Terah, had intended to go in the first place? For another five hundred miles they moved south in a slow trudging caravan, passing Damascus, the world's oldest existing city.

They stopped at Shechem, where the Canaanites lived. The gently sloping hills were green with thick grass and the higher mountains were covered with graceful, fragrant cypress trees. Sarai was happy. She liked the land and wanted to settle there. But she would not utter her wish to Abram. She had to follow her husband.

Abram knew that unless the Lord himself showed him the land, he could not take it. He built an altar on the hillside and made a sacrifice. While praying, the Lord spoke to him again, "To your seed I will give this land."

Abram could not understand how God would give this land to his seed. He was already seventy-five. His wife Sarai was not a young woman either, and they were still childless. But God said it and so be it, thought Abram fully confident.

When they came to Bethel Abram pitched another tent. Once again he built an altar for sacrifice. Lot was married now to a quick tempered, impatient woman. They both were tired and restless from the long sojourn over dusty roads. But this place was not destined for them either. Soon they learned that Canaan was enduring a severe famine. They set on the road again.

It was a long trek across the Arabian Desert to Egypt. While the people of the desert and in the land north of it were still nomads, Egypt had developed into a political nation. To the Egyptians, Abram appeared to be a wandering sheik. Since it was such a large group of people with many servants and a long camel train, the Egyptians were curious to know why they had come and what their intentions were.

Abram feared for his own life. Talking with the first Egyptians they met — the Pharaoh's guard — he noticed them looking with delight at Sarai. Quickly, he decided to use his wife as a shield for his protection, whispering to Sarai.

> *You are a woman beautiful to behold. When the Egyptian ruler sees you they will kill me. Tell them that you are my sister, that my life can be spared on your account.*

Being a dutiful wife, Sarai did not object. When the Pharaoh saw her—tall and slender of stature, long brown hair twined in braids on her head like a crown, a beautiful oval face, blue eyes shadowed under the eyelashes—his eyes gleamed in admiration. He asked to whom the woman belonged and, pointing at Abram, Sarai answered, "I am his sister."

Sarai was taken to the Pharaoh's house. In exchange for his wife, Abram received generous gifts: sheep, oxen, asses, camels and servants. Abram was indeed a rich man.

But the Lord God was not pleased. He sent great plagues to the land of Egypt because of Sarai. God also warned Pharaoh in a dream. Abram was summoned to the palace and Pharaoh asked him,

> *Why did you not tell me that she was your wife?*
> *Why did you say, 'she is my sister' so that I took*
> *her for my wife?*

Pharaoh, fearing the God of Abram, gave back Sarai and all the riches which Abram had acquired during his stay in Egypt. Abram took his possessions, Sarai, Lot and Lot's family, and left Egypt. He headed back to Bethel. His tent was still there. This meant that he had claimed the land and it belonged to him.

For some time life in Bethel went smoothly. When the grass of the best pastures was gone, Lot's shepherds got into frequent arguments with Abram's flock keepers about the choice of grazing land. Abram did not want any misunderstanding among his kinsmen.

One day Lot went to Abram's tent to talk things over. Abram, treating him very fatherly, said:

> *Let there be no strife between you and me, for we*
> *are kinsmen. Take the land of your choice and sep-*
> *arate from me.*

Lot, taking with him his family, cattle, servants and all their belongings, left for the well-watered valley of the Jordan in the direction of Zoar.

There were several cities in this fertile land. One of them was Sodom and another, Gomorrah. After several years of camping in one place and then moving on to another, Lot settled in Sodom.

After Lot departed, Abram took down his tents and moved to Hebron. There he built an altar of field stones and raised a tent above it. Now he thought he would live in peace. He did, but for only a few years. He often wondered how his kin fared in the far-off city of Sodom. One day travelers from a passing caravan told him that Sodom had been attacked by enemies who took Lot away and locked him in prison.

Abram was not a man of war. He loved peace and practiced

it, but the news upset him immensely. He invoked aid from Heaven and, gathering his servants and whatever tools he had, he surprised the enemy by attack and freed his kinsman. Lot was very grateful and regretted having separated from his uncle.

Abram did not waste any time. As soon as the battle was over and Lot freed from prison, he set out for home. On the way the entire caravan was stopped while passing outside of Salem, also called Jeru-Salem, "place of peace," later known as Jerusalem.

To the city gates of Salem came the king—the priest Melchizedec—to greet Abram. The holy man Melchizedek worshipped one God, the Most High. He recognized Abram as God's chosen father of many nations and, as such, bestowed on him a great honor, blessing him with bread and wine, foreshadowing the Blessed Sacrament of ages to come. He bestowed on Abram his priestly blessing, "Blessed be Abram by God Most High!"

On the altar a sacrifice was made, not a burnt one, but a new kind, of bread and wine, portent of the New Covenant at the Last Supper.

Abram gave a tenth of all he had to the High Priest Melchizedek, exclaiming, "You are a priest forever!" The prophet and the patriarch bid each other good-bye with an embrace.

Abram returned to Hebron. His warriors grumbled because Abram refused to allow them to carry off any loot from the field of battle. But God's voice once again spoke to Abram, saying:

Fear not, Abram, I am your shield; your reward shall be great, for I will multiply your descendants.

This time Abram complained to God:

O Lord God, what will you give me, for I continue childless and the heir of my house is Eliezer.

Eliezer, whose parents came from Damascus, was the steward of the slaves in Abram's household.

The Voice replied, "This man shall not be your heir." Leading Abram outside of his tent, the Voice continued, "look toward heaven and number the stars. So shall your descendants be."

On that day the Lord God made a covenant with Abram. "To your descendants I give this land, from the River of Egypt to the great River Euphrates."

Abram told Sarai about the covenant. Upon hearing the message she became agitated and blamed herself for being an obstacle to God's plan. Her inability to be the mother of Abram's children was a constant pain in her heart. She took it upon herself to find a way to fulfill God's promise.

Sarai had an Egyptian maid named Hagar. She was young and healthy, and there was no doubt about her fertility.

"Take my maid Hagar," suggested Sarai.

"Hagar?" questioned Abram with surprise. Until now he had hardly noticed the Egyptian slave.

As Hagar passed the tent in front of which Abram sat, he looked closely at the servant girl. Her eyes were as brown and oval as coconuts from the valley of the Nile. Her bronze skin had a healthy sheen and, when her red lips parted, her white teeth sparkled. The servant's body was barely covered and its rhythmic motions were graceful. It was not against the custom in those days to have a mistress and Hagar's youth and vigor was very appealing, even to conscientious Abram.

One evening, when everyone was retiring, he entered the tent of Hagar.

It did not take long to notice that Hagar was with child. As the warm days of spring increased, so too increased Hagar's self-esteem. Her bearing had an air of importance and, instead of being a servant girl to Sarai, she felt more and more like the mother of Abram's expected child, more important than Sarai. She did not fail to show it whenever she had the opportunity. This irritated Sarai and she complained to Abram. Abram, being a peaceful man, tried to calm down his wife, saying "Be patient with her."

But Sarai was losing her patience. The relationship between the two women became unbearably strained by the resentment each had for the other. Sarai in her jealousy dealt harshly with her slave girl, causing Hagar to flee into the wilderness. There, by the spring

"Return to your mistress Sarai," said the angel.

of water next to which Hagar collapsed from exhaustion, an angel of the Lord appeared to her, saying, "Hagar, maid of Sarai, where are you going?"

"I am fleeing from my mistress Sarai," complained Hagar.

"Return to your mistress," said the angel. "And submit to her. I will multiply your descendants so that they can not be numbered for multitude. You will bear a son and call him Ishmael. He will be a wild man and against every man."

Hagar was visibly shaken. She knew that God had spoken to Abram, the father of the child she was carrying, but, that God found her worthy to speak to, was beyond her comprehension. On her knees, arms crossed over her full bosom, she cried, "You are the God of seeing!"

It took her some time to return to her senses. She repeated many times to herself, "Have I really seen God and remained alive after seeing him?"

There was only one thing for her to do now. Getting up, she trudged back through the hot desert sand, full with child, barefoot, hungry and thirsty, to the tents of Abram and Sarai. Upon return she submitted to the demands of her jealous mistress, being obedient to the Voice of God and regarding it as a great treasure in her womanly heart.

Hagar bore Abram a son, just as it was prophesied. Abram was happy and very proud of his son. He named him Ishmael, meaning "God hears."

Four years later God appeared to Abram saying, "I am God Almighty; walk before me and be blameless. And I will make a covenant between me and you and will multiply you exceedingly."

Abram fell to the ground on his face. The Voice continued by telling him that he, Abram, would be the father of many nations. From this time forward he would be called not mere Abram but Abraham, which means "father of multitude." From him would come kings and there would be an everlasting covenant between God and Abraham's descendants. Also, his wife Sarai from then on would be called Sarah, meaning "a great lady." "I will bless her and I will give you a son by her; she will be a mother of nations, kings of peoples shall come from her."

Abraham, still laying face down on the ground, reflected to himself about what God said, "Shall a child be born to a man who is a hundred years old? Shall Sarah who is ninety bear a child?" Remembering his son born to Hagar, he lifted his head from the ground and called out to God, "Oh, that Ishmael might live in thy sight!"

But this was not what God meant.

"No, but Sarah, your wife, shall bear a son and you shall call his name Isaac."

Abraham, obedient to God's will all of his life, did not ask any more questions.

A visible sign of this covenant between God and Abraham was to be the circumcision of every male child when eight days old and every male living in Abraham's time. A command was a command for Abraham. He set to work immediately. First he circumcized his son Ishmael, then he performed the painful surgery on himself and on every male in his household.

8. The Trial of Love

On a summer day in Mamre, under the large oak tree in front of his tent, Abraham sat resting in the heat of the afternoon. Many travelers passed his tent since it was located alongside of the road. Abraham was deep in prayer. He raised his eyes to heaven and saw a sunbeam across the blue sky, nearly touching the earth. That reminded him of Noah and the rainbow, when the first covenant between God and man was made. The stories which he heard from travelers horrified him. Abraham prayed for the redemption of mankind.

When he finished praying he saw three men approaching his tent. They were dressed in white girded garments. Upon seeing them, something stirred in Abraham's heart. He hurried to meet them. Bowing low, he asked them not to pass his tent, but rather to stay with him and take a rest. The three strangers accepted the invitation. Abraham rushed to his wife, giving her orders to prepare a banquet for the noble guests. A fatling was slaughtered and an elaborate meal was set on the table. While the guests were eating, Abraham stood by serving them under the oak tree.

The strangers foretold to Abraham the birth of his son Isaac. Sarah, out of curiosity, was inside listening to their talk. When she heard about the birth of a son, she burst into laughter.

The strangers heard her and asked, "Why did Sarah laugh and say, 'Shall I indeed bear a child, now that I am old?' Is not everything possible with God?"

But Sarah, hearing this from behind the door, became frightened and called, "I did not laugh."

But the man replied, "No, but you did laugh."

The three strangers were ready to leave. Abraham, embarassed by Sarah, but still glad and trusting about the promise of a son, accompanied the men some distance from his dwelling. On the hill he pointed out the direction of Sodom since the men said that they were on the way to Sodom and Gomorrah. Before bidding goodbye the strangers told him that the outcry against Sodom and Gomorrah was so great that they were on their way there to destroy the two cities.

The three men departed, but Abraham could not move from the spot. Wasn't his nephew Lot and his other kin in Sodom? What would become of them?

The only thing Abraham knew to do was to turn to God in prayer.

"Will you indeed destroy the righteous with the wicked? Far be it from thee! If there are fifty righteous people would you spare the place?"

"If I find fifty righteous people I will spare the whole city for their sake," promised the Lord.

But Abraham became frightened and began thinking that if there were not fifty who follow the Lord, what then? He began haggling with God—forty-five, thirty, twenty, ten—and the Lord was willing to spare the city if there were only ten God-fearing people in it.

When the two angels came to the city of Sodom they found only one just man—Lot. And God remembered Abraham's plea to spare at least the just ones if there weren't ten righteous people. An angel told Lot to take his wife and two daughters and flee the city. He warned them to run as fast as they could and not look back.

The night was very dark and, as soon as they were out of the city and had reached the first hill, the Lord rained brimstone and fire on Sodom and Gomorrah. The earth shook violently from explosions.

Lot's wife, unable to resist the temptation, looked back over her shoulder. At that moment, she became a pillar of salt.

Both cities were completely destroyed and erased from the face of the earth, along with all of the inhabitants in them. Even from the great distance, Abraham saw the destruction of Sodom and Gomorrah. He knew confidently, though, that Lot was spared.

Soon after that Sarah had glorious news for Abraham—she was with child. When the boy was born, Abraham named him Isaac, meaning "joy," just as the Lord had foretold.

By this time Ishmael had grown into a tall handsome lad. When Sarah saw him playing with Isaac she became jealous and nagged Abraham to cast out the boy and his mother Hagar. "The son of this slave woman shall not be heir with my son Isaac," she objected.

Abraham was sad and did not know what to do, until the Voice told him to do what Sarah wanted. "I will make a nation of the slave woman's son also, because he is your offspring," promised the Lord.

Hagar was forced to leave. With a few loaves of bread and a skin filled with water, she headed, hand in hand with her teenage son, into the wilderness of the desert for a second time. When all the bread was eaten and there was no more water, the boy fainted, exhausted from the heat and thirst. Hagar tried to revive him but all her efforts were in vain. The boy could not walk any longer and he was much too heavy to be carried by his mother whose strength was drained also.

Not able to face the death of her child, Hagar moved farther away from the boy. After a while she heard the boy's weak moaning. Then she heard a voice. It was unmistakably the Voice that made her return to Sarah when she was carrying the child under her heart

"What troubles you, Hagar," asked the Voice. "Fear not; for God has heard the voice of the lad. Arise, lift up the lad and hold him fast with your hand; for I will make him a great nation."

When Hagar opened her eyes she saw a well nearby, which wasn't there before. She filled the skin with water and gave her son a drink. From then on Hagar knew that the Lord was with her and her son.

Soon they found a village called Paran. There they lived until Ishmael grew to be a man, skilled in archery. He married an Egyptian girl, like his mother. Following in his father's footsteps, he circumcised his sons in the same manner that Abraham had circumcised him.

Abraham missed his son Ishmael. He thought about him frequently. His sole consolation was God's promise to take care of Ishmael and, like always, Abraham trusted God's word.

Years passed and Isaac grew from infancy into boyhood. He was a child of calm temper, always happy and gentle. Abraham loved his son dearly and spent a great deal of time with him. Isaac was eleven years old and was constantly at his father's side. He gave so much joy to Abraham in his old age that God took his faithful servant to test.

"Abraham," called the Lord one afternoon.

"Here I am," answered the old man.

"Take your son Isaac whom you love, and go to the land of Moriah. Offer him there as a burnt sacrifice."

Abraham could not believe his own ears. Isaac, the promised

son, the joy of his old age whom he loved more than anything, had to be sacrificed as a lamb on the altar! How could he do it? There was no mistake, though. The God Almighty, to whom Abraham was obedient all his life, had spoken.

All night long Abraham could not sleep. No matter how he tried to reason, it made no sense. "God is asking the greatest possible sacrifice of me. Haven't I waited a hundred years for this promised son? Didn't God himself say that from this son a great nation would be made? Doesn't God know that I love Isaac? Yes, he does," Abraham continued to muse. "He said, 'take your son Isaac, whom you love.' Lord, let me die instead. I am an old man." But the Voice was silent. God was testing Abraham's love and Abraham knew it.

When dawn first lightened the eastern sky, Abraham was still wrestling with himself. "Whom do I love more—my son Isaac or God? Wasn't it God who gave me Isaac? Hasn't he the right to take him when he wants?"

The trial was over in Abraham's soul. In a loud voice he called to his servants, "Get up! We are leaving for Moriah to worship the Almighty!"

With heavy heart and deep grief Abraham began preparing for the journey. He took two menservants, Isaac and an ass. They headed north from Beersheba towards the heights of Moriah, one of seven mountains on which Jerusalem was built.

All the way Abraham did not speak even one word. This seemed rather unusual to Isaac, but since they were going to worship, the menservants and Isaac respected Abraham's silence. They walked for three days until Abraham saw the appointed mountain in the distance. There he told the menservants to wait. Taking the kindling wood from the ass, he put it on the back of his young healthy son Isaac, and only the two of them continued to climb to the top of Mount Moriah.

Alone with his father, Isaac took courage to ask him a question, "Father, behold the fire and the wood, but where is the lamb for sacrifice?"

"God himself will provide," answered Abraham, not raising his eyes to Isaac.

They both climbed the mountain — Isaac, with the load of wood on his back, to be offered as a lamb on the altar of love and Abraham with a hidden knife and grief-stricken heart.

On top of the mountain was a large rock on which Abraham laid the wood. Isaac again asked, "Where is the sacrificial lamb?"

Abraham looked at his good son and, for the first time, Isaac understood. Being obedient, just like his father, Isaac did not struggle. He stretched out his arms to be tied up. Abraham bound Isaac and laid him upon the altar. Taking a long knife from his belt, Abraham lifted it up to slay his son before burning. At this moment the Voice of the Lord called,

"Abraham! Abraham!"

"Here I am, Lord!"

"Do not lay your hand on the lad. Because you acted as you did, in not withholding from me your beloved son, I will bless you abundantly."

A ram was bleating in the thicket nearby. Freed from the ropes, Isaac ran to bring it for sacrifice. While the offering burned, father and son stood by the altar completely enwrapped in prayer. Then, hand in hand, full of joy praising the Lord, they descended the hill. They joined the menservants at the bottom and together returned to Beersheba.

9. The Parents of Two Nations

Sarah—mother of only one son, Isaac—parted from life at the age of one hundred twenty-seven.* Abraham mourned his beloved wife.

East of Mamre he bought a field with a cave on the premises. In it he buried Sarah. Left alone, he completely depended on Isaac. Although Isaac was a grown man, he was constantly in his father's

"Do not lay your hand on the lad!"

company. Both men were of similar character, peace loving, mild mannered and living in harmony and faith.

But one day Abraham became concerned about the situation and told his son it was time for him to marry. Although Abraham knew how much Isaac loved him, he did not expect him to spend all his life at his father's side. Wasn't he forty already and still single? The only problem was to find the right woman! Abraham did not care much for Canaanite women and decided his chosen son's wife should come from among his own people in Mesopotamia.

Abraham called his trusted servant Eliezer and made him swear that he would bring Isaac a wife from Abraham's kin. Eliezer left for Nahor in distant Mesopotamia and brought Isaac a beautiful girl, Rebekah. When Isaac and Rebekah saw each other they were pleasantly surprised and fell in love with one another.

Rebekah loved her father-in-law, Abraham, with a filial affection and she enjoyed his company just as much as Isaac did. Not wanting to depend on his son completely, Abraham got himself a wife. Her name was Keturah.

Years passed quickly. God blessed Keturah, giving Abraham children even in his old age. Rebekah, sharing Sarah's fate, remained childless. Abraham tried to console her, but who can console a barren woman's heart?

Meantime, Keturah had one son after another. Rebekah became more and more depressed. The house was filled with the sound of Abraham and Keturah's sons.

Often in the cool of the evening Abraham and Rebekah sat outside their tents resting and talking peacefully after the day's work. Abraham would look towards the sky and remember God's promise to multiply his descendants as the stars in the sky. On one such evening Abraham thanked God, in quiet gratitude, for his blessing, and, with joy and excitement, he related to Rebekah the glad news. Keturah was expecting his sixth child!

---

*She is the only woman whose age is given in the Bible.

Tears streaming down her cheeks, Rebekah cried in distress. It seemed cruelly unfair. Keturah had a child every year . . . why not she? Now, since Ishmael joined them after Sarah's death, his wife also had many children, all husky and rowdy boys just like their father. She, Rebekah, was the only one whom God refused to make fruitful.

Abraham understood this young woman's anguish only too well. He remembered his own Sarah who was so difficult to console in her barren years.

"Rebekah," Abraham spoke soothingly, "remember Sarah. She conceived Isaac when she was ninety-five and you are only forty." Abraham chuckled at the thought of comparison, but Rebekah did not find it amusing. She wanted a child and did not have the patience to wait another fifty years.

Abraham was an old man now. All he possessed he gave to Isaac, his heir. To the children of his other wives he gave gifts and sent them away eastward. God's blessing rested upon Isaac, and Abraham knew that the lineage of chosen people was to be continued in him.

At the age of one hundred and seventy-five, Abraham did not wake up one morning. Isaac and Ishmael stood side by side mourning their father. They buried him next to his wife Sarah in the cave of Machepelah at the foot of Mount Hebron, east of Mamre.

So great was Rebekah's bereavement for her father-in-law that Isaac looked upon her with compassion. Now, since Abraham's children were also gone, the house was deathly quiet, empty and eerie.

Rebekah wanted to get away, away from the land which refused to bless her with offspring. She nagged Isaac with more and more demands each day.

Isaac, however, dearly loved the land of his father. He felt he belonged in this place—here were his friends, his kin. Here were buried his mother and father. Why should he leave? Where should he go?

He went to the field to be alone. There Isaac prayed for a long time in mute silence. Then he heard the Voice quietly speaking in his heart, "Go to the land of Rebekah's birth and I will bless you and her."

They moved to Nahor. The changed surroundings which created many new tasks, helped turn Rebekah's mind away from herself. Her interest in others made her a happier person. She was again a tender wife to Isaac, as in the first years of their marriage.

One evening when Isaac returned home from his daily chores in the fields, he noticed an even greater change in Rebekah. He thought to himself, "She is as beautiful as the day Eliezer brought her for my bride!"

Rebekah rushed to greet Isaac, her eyes filled with tears of joy. Embracing her husband, she told him joyous tidings, "Isaac, the Lord has blessed me. I am with child!"

Great was their joy, and they praised the Lord, the God of Abraham, the God of Noah and the Creator of Adam. Rebekah remembered the faith of Abraham, his words of encouragement and how he compared her fate to Sarah's. Repenting her dismay, she thanked God the Father with even deeper gratitude for the favor she received.

From the moment Isaac's seed stirred in her womb, Rebekah's peace of mind and body was gone. She felt a lot of activity in her womb and it became greater with each day. Before long the midwives told her that she was carrying a set of violently kicking twins. The two unborn children were so active and made such a tumult in Rebekah's body that all assembled midwives and nurses said they had never known anything like it! The twins rolled and turned, kicked and elbowed so much that it seemed they were struggling with each other. The tumbling prevented her from sleeping and she became exhausted and quite upset from the unrest.

Weeks passed in troubled anguish, until Rebekah, saddened by what was going on and unable to find a solution anywhere, turned to God in prayer. The Lord heard her cries and, in compassion, told her:

Two nations are in your womb, and two peoples, born of you, shall be divided; the one shall be stronger than the other, the elder shall serve the younger.

The first-born of the twins was a red-skinned boy, all covered with thick hair. They called him Esau*. He was followed by his brother holding Esau's heel. They called him Jacob**.

From the very beginning, the boys were not only completely different in looks and temperament, but also rivals. Esau grew up to be a hunter, strong, robust and quick-tempered. He was just like his uncle Ishmael. Jacob was gentle and slower in motion, but much quicker of mind.

Isaac favored Esau. He was attracted by his older son's ruggedness and vigor, just the opposite of himself and his younger son. Often Esau would bring home game and prepare a spiced savory meal, just as Isaac loved. While Isaac ate, Esau would tell him the wildest stories of his hunting jaunts. In his old age Isaac found these stories amusing and entertaining and never tired of hearing them.

Jacob was favored by his mother. Rebekah was a determined woman. She relied on the Voice of God during her pregnancy and decided that the ruler of the house should not be the older one, who had the birthright for it, but the younger one who was far more intelligent. He would rule people and possessions not by force and harshness, but rather in a wise manner with fairness and justice.

One day when Jacob was cooking pottage in the field, Esau returned from a hunting trip. He was tired and hungry. Wiping his sweating face with his hairy arm, Esau smelled the aroma of food temptingly steaming from the cooking pot.

He pleaded with his brother, "Give me some of that red pottage for I am famished!"

---

*This meant "red."
**This meant "one who supplants."

Jacob looked at his big red-headed brother and teased him, "If I give you enough to satisfy your hunger, there will be none left for myself!"

"But, Brother, I'll give you whatever you want in exchange for this dish of stew."

"Even your birthright?" Jacob asked cunningly.

"What good is a birthright to me," exclaimed Esau, "if I am dying from hunger?"

This was the talk of an indulgent boy and not a man. Jacob wanted to make a firm deal, so that his brother could not change his mind later and say that the whole thing was only a joke. He shrewdly said to Esau, "Swear to me first!"

"Why all this ado about such a little thing when I feel as though I am starving to death?" Esau wondered to himself. He just wanted to get over with all the trifling ceremonies so that he could eat and save his life! Saliva filling the corners of his mouth, Esau hastily swore.

Jacob gave Esau his savory red bean meal, along with several pieces of bread and a cup of hearty wine. He served him royally.

After Esau satisfied his enormous appetite, he took a good long nap. It was then that Jacob hurried home and told Rebekah what had happened. Overjoyed and excited, mother and son joined hands and danced blissfully around the room.

What was done, was done. Mother and son never mentioned it again. Only, Rebekah's step was even more self-assured, her face seemingly happier and her mind shrewder.

Isaac was getting very old. His eyesight was failing and all he could see were dim shadows. The time came for him to bestow his blessing on his son before getting too feeble. Rebekah watched him very closely. She was determined not to permit anything to slip by her attentive sight. They discussed and even argued many times about which son should get the blessing. But Isaac disregarded Rebekah's feelings toward her favorite, Jacob. The first-born should have the blessing, and to him it would be given, was the unwavering decision of the old patriarch.

Thinking they were alone one day, Isaac said to Esau: "My son, take your weapons—your quiver and bow—and go out to the field and hunt some game. Then prepare a savory meal such as I love, and I will bless you."

Rebekah, listening through the thin walls of the tent, heard what Isaac said to their older son. As soon as Esau left, she called in Jacob and instructed him hurriedly, "Go to the flock and fetch me two fat kids so that I can prepare from them a savory meal for your father. You will give it him and he will bless you instead of Esau."

With deep anxiety Rebekah had awaited this moment for many years. Now that it had arrived, she was extremely tense.

"But mother," objected the worried Jacob, "Esau is a hairy man and I am a smooth man. Perhaps father will feel me and, thinking I am mocking him, he will curse me."

"Upon me then be your curse, my son. Just do what I say!"

Jacob left without a chance to ask Rebekah what Esau would do when he found out. "But didn't he sell his birthright for a dish of pottage?" mused Jacob. The agreement was irrevocable so Jacob decided not to worry about Esau.

Jacob fetched two fatlings and, when the meal was ready, Rebekah pulled out of the chest the best of Esau's garments and put it on Jacob. Then she tied the skins of the kids on his arms and chest, since the garment had a slit in front, leaving the chest exposed.

With the hot dish in his shaky hands, Jacob entered Isaac's tent. Approaching his father's bed, Jacob tried to imitate his brother's voice.

"My father," said Jacob in the changed voice.

"Who are you, my son?" asked nearly blind Isaac.

"I am your son Esau. I have done as you told me. Sit up and eat, that you may bless me."

Isaac, although old and unable to see, was fully alert in his mind. He sensed right away that something was wrong.

"How did you find the game so quickly?" he questioned his nervous son.

"The Lord your God granted me success," lied Jacob.

"Come near me so that I may feel you," instructed Isaac whose doubts were mounting higher.

Jacob came close to his father and kneeled down. Isaac touched his son's outstretched arms which were covered with the skins of a kid, then his chest. Still uncertain, Isaac thought out loud: "The voice is Jacob's, but the arms are Esau's. Are you really my son Esau?"

"I am," replied Jacob in a trembling voice.

Full of doubts, Isaac ate his meal of tasty meat and drank the wine that Jacob brought him. Then he addressed his son again.

"Come nearer and kiss me, my son."

Jacob bent over his father and kissed him. Isaac smelled the hunter's clothes which have such a distinct odor, especially for a blind man's sensitive smell. Now he was satisfied — for he had smelled Esau's garments. He blessed his kneeling son with the most important blessing.

> *May God give you of the dew of heaven, and of the*
> *fatness of the earth, and plenty of grain and wine.*
> *Let peoples serve you, and nations bow down to*
> *you. Be lord over your brothers, and may your*
> *mother's sons bow down to you. Cursed be every*
> *one who curses you, and blessed be every one who*
> *blesses you!*

When the blessing was over, Isaac, tired and feeble, leaned back on his pillows and dozed. Jacob slipped out of the tent. Crossing the yard to his mother's tent Jacob heard a familiar whistle. Esau, full of confidence, was returning from the hunt, his game tossed over his shoulder. He prepared a savory repast and brought it to his father.

Hearing Esau's voice and realizing what had happened, Isaac, was shocked. Trembling all over he asked, "Whom did I bless before you came? Yes, and he will be blessed."

"Bless me too, my father!" pleaded Esau anxiously.

"Your brother came with guile," told the saddened patriarch, "and took your blessing."

"Don't you have another blessing for me?" the older brother cried bitterly.

Instead of a blessing, Isaac gave his first-born a prophecy: "By your sword you shall live," said Isaac in a very dejected voice. "You shall serve your brother until you shall break his yoke from your neck."

Enraged, Esau left Isaac's tent. To a manservant passing by, he said, "The days of mourning for my father are approaching, then I will kill my brother Jacob."

Rebekah, hearing Esau's intention, did not waste any time. She promptly called Jacob and told him to leave immediately for her brother's house.

"Stay there until your brother's fury is appeased," she warned.

This was the last time Jacob saw his dearly loved mother. Early in the morning he left Beersheba alone, on foot, with only what he could carry on his back.

10. Jacob and Laban

The sun beating down on his head, Jacob walked over the hills and valleys all day, not daring to stop for a rest. At sunset he climbed to the top of a hill and sat on a rock. He was too tired to travel any farther. Putting down his sack containing some loaves of bread and a jug of wine, he took a look around himself. There was a magnificent view from this hill. Soon stars appeared in the clear sky. Jacob made himself a bed by turning over a stone on which to lay his head, heavy with thoughts about the uncertain future.

During that night Jacob had a mysterious dream, a dream that stunned the runaway. In his dream he saw a ladder set up on earth with the top of it reaching up to heaven. Angels were ascending and descending the ladder. On top of it was the Lord God. Jacob heard the deep voice of the Lord which was so familiar to Abraham, his grandfather.

"I am the Lord, the God of Abraham and your father, Isaac," the Voice proclaimed. "The land on which you lie I will give to you and your descendants. . . . Behold, I am with you and will keep you wherever you go."

Jacob awoke deeply puzzled. The Lord, he who knows and sees everything, surely knew how he had cheated his brother out of his legitimate birthright and blessing. How could God forgive him, much less bless him?

"Surely the Lord is in this place and I did not know it," he said soberly.

A revelation is often painful and it usually ends in soul-searching and contrition. When God reveals himself, one's reaction is either like that of the Roman centurion, "Lord, I am not worthy," or of Peter, "Depart from me for I am a sinful man," or of humble submittance as was true of the unbelieving Thomas' response, "My Lord and my God!"

God's revelation was completely baffling to Jacob. Falling on the ground, he prayed for forgiveness realizing his unworthiness in the face of the Lord. Then he consecrated himself to the service of God, sincerely promising: "If I am really chosen, Lord, from now on I will give myself wholly to your service."

Getting up, he took the stone on which he had layed his head and placed it upright. Then he poured some oil on it and named the place Bethel, which means "be blessed." There he made a vow: "If God will be with me, this stone, which I set up for a pillar, shall be God's house!"

Jacob resumed his journey toward Haran. On his way he joined some shepherds. He asked them if they knew Laban, the son of Nahor. They surely did and, even more, they said to him, "Look! Here comes Rachel, Laban's daughter. She is the one with the sheep."

Jacob saw Rachel, the daughter of his mother's brother. Even from a distance he could discern her beauty. Hurrying to her, he embraced Rachel with a kiss. Rachel stood dumbfounded, staring at the handsome stranger. Jacob explained that he was her cousin from distant Canaan.

At this moment, love was kindled in their hearts. Their deep affection for each other lasted lifelong.

Laban greeted Jacob with open arms, as a kinsman should be received. Laban, though, was a cunning man. Instead of worshipping one God, the God of Adam and Abraham, he worshipped man-made idols.

Seeing that Jacob's visit would be prolonged, Laban was puzzled about his kinsman's intentions. One day he approached Jacob shrewdly, "Although we are kinsmen, you should not serve me for nothing. Tell me. What shall your wages be?"

"I will serve you seven years in exchange for your younger daughter Rachel," exclaimed Jacob out of heartfelt generosity. In gratitude for God's revelation, Jacob was ready for atonement.

Planning ahead, Laban agreed. An ugly smirk came across his wrinkled red face as he chuckled to himself. He had two daughters. The older one, Leah, was a bleary-eyed girl with neither the poise nor beauty of Rachel. She always squinted her reddish watery eyes, making herself look even less attractive. No suitors sought Leah for a wife.

When seven years elapsed, Jacob asked Laban to give him Rachel as his wife.

Laban prepared a lavish wedding feast, inviting all his relatives and neighbors. That evening, according to local custom, the bride was brought in covered from head to toe with many veils.

The next morning, when the first sunrays penetrated the newlyweds' tent, Jacob woke up. With one arm under his bride's head and embracing her with the other, he tenderly looked at her. As soon as he saw her face, he left out a shrill cry. Next to him was not his beloved Rachel but her older sister, homely looking Leah!

Jumping to his feet, Jacob ran to Laban.

"What have you done to me?" he demanded of his father-in-law. "Did I not serve you for Rachel? Why did you deceive me?"

Old Laban chuckled wilily, "Don't you know our custom that the older daughter has to be given in marriage first and only then, the younger one? Serve me another seven years and I'll give Rachel for your wife also."

Rachel was the only one he wanted. His love for her was worth far more than the sweat and toil of seven additional years. Jacob agreed to accept Laban's proposition.

Although homely in appearance, Leah was very sensitive. She needed and deeply desired love from her husband. She knew full well that Jacob's eyes were always dwelling on Rachel. Leah was extremely jealous.

God has a seemingly strange way of dealing with his selected ones. Leah was given to Jacob as a punishment and, at the same time, as a blessing.

When seven more years had passed, Rachel became Jacob's wife. Now there was no end to Leah's laments because Jacob loved only Rachel. Leah cried frequently. Although Jacob was insensitive to her sorrow, God heard her crying and blessed her with one son after another, while Rachel remained barren. Now there was reason for Rachel to be envious.

"Give me children or I shall die!" sobbed Rachel to Jacob.

Jacob, shocked at his wife's blasphemy, angrily retorted, "Am I in the place of God, who has withheld from you the fruit of the womb?"

In her distress Rachel gave Jacob her maid, Bilah. Bilah had two sons by Jacob.

Leah, seeing this, immediately entered into competition with her rival sister by giving Jacob her own servant girl, Zilpah. Zilpah, also, had two sons. Leah thought she could win her husband's love by giving him many sons. With every child she conceived, she hoped that its birth would turn Jacob's heart to her. She gave Jacob six sons and a daughter, Dinah.

The consolation which her two sons born to Bilah brought Rachel seemed to calm her down quite a bit. But, her greatest joy was the discovery that she herself was with child! When the boy was born she called him Joseph,* saying "May the Lord add to me another son!"

Jacob was happy, happy for Rachel as well as himself, and grateful beyond reason to the Lord for the birth of his beloved son Joseph. From the time of conception he loved this child more than any other of his sons, because he loved Rachel more than any other woman.

God had blessed Jacob in every way. He not only fathered many children but also was a man of great wealth. Regardless of all the success he had, there was a constant pang in his heart. As the years advanced, he felt its pain more sharply. He longed more and more for his father's home, for the land of his birth and youth. He became even more disheartened when he realized that Laban was repeatedly cheating him on wages. He wanted to get away and be on his own. But, how? With the responsibility of eleven sons, (daughters were not even counted in those days), four wives, servants and large herds of cattle, it would not be an easy decision. Besides, what if his wives, Laban's daughters, were to say they did not want to leave their father to face the unknown without any promise of security?

In the midst of his frustrations, Jacob had another dream. The Voice spoke to him again.

"Jacob!" called the Voice.

"Here I am," responded Jacob.

"I have seen all that Laban is doing to you," the Voice related. "I am the God of Bethel, where you anointed a pillar and made a

---

*That in Hebrew means "He adds."

vow to me. Now arise, go forth from this land and return to the land of your birth."

Jacob called a family council. He explained his dream to both his wives, Leah and Rachel. The air of importance and sobriety in their husband's voice impressed both women, and they agreed to heed the will of God.

"Whatever God has said for you to do, do," both Leah and Rachel advised Jacob.

Having already been cheated by Laban ten times, Jacob decided not to take any chances this time. While Laban was off shearing sheep in distant fields, Jacob gave the order to start packing so as to be ready to depart at dawn.

In the hurry-scurry of packing, Rachel, nevertheless, felt quite perplexed. Joseph was now a small boy, but would the Lord bless her again? Would the new place be a fruitful one for her? Among her father's household belongings, was an image of the pagan god of fertility. She had no problem sneaking into her father's tent and taking the statue.

When Laban returned home and saw that Jacob had left with his household, he was infuriated. He gathered his sons and men-servants and together they pursued Jacob for seven days. In the hill country of Gilead he caught sight of the fugitives. But, by night, God came to Laban in a dream.

"Take heed that you say not one word to Jacob, either good or bad," warned the Voice.

Laban overtook Jacob on Mount Gilead. Because of the dream, he did not dare attack him. Instead he decided to use his wits, cunningly asking Jacob:

"Why didn't you tell me you longed so much for your father's house? I would have sent you away with mirth and songs, with tambourine and lyre. Why did you not permit me to kiss my sons and daughters farewell? You have acted foolishly. And, why did you steal my gods?"

Jacob had many lessons from his father-in-law. He knew Laban's nature quite well.

"I was afraid you would take your daughters from me by force." Having no idea that his beloved Rachel was hiding a false god in her saddlebag, Jacob continued, "Anyone with whom you find your gods shall not live."

Very carefully Laban searched every tent and person. Rachel, astride her camel, said to her father, "Let not my lord be angry that I cannot rise before you, for the way of women is upon me."

When Laban did not find the statue of the household god Jacob became angry with him.

"What is my sin that you have so boldly pursued me?" retorted Jacob. "I served you fourteen years in exchange for your two daughters and another six years for your flock. You changed my wages ten times. If the God of Abraham and the fear of Isaac had not been on my side, you surely would have sent me away empty-handed. God saw my affliction and rebuked you last night."

Laban was not a man to give in easily and, by no means, wanted to be a loser. If he could not take away possessions, at least he would put himself in good light by showing how tolerant he was.

"The daughters are my daughters and all you see is mine," replied Laban. Then, opening his arms wide, he continued in honey-eyed tones, "But what can I do with all that? Come now, let us make a covenant, you and I."

They gathered a heap of stones and made an altar, as a sign in witness to their agreement. Jacob offered a sacrifice on that altar, praising the God of Abraham and the God of Isaac. All their kinsmen were standing around the altar. After the sacrifice Jacob asked all his in-laws to share bread with him. They tarried on the mountain all night, talking and singing together in mutual love and peace.

Next morning Laban said good-bye, kissing his grandchildren and daughters. Giving his fatherly blessing to them, Laban parted from them and returned to Nahor, his home.

11. Israel — Father of the Twelve Tribes

Being rid of Laban was a relief for Jacob, but his peace of mind did not last for a long time. Worried about settling accounts with his twin brother Esau, Jacob set out to find him. Straddling the lead camel of his long trudging caravan, Jacob saw a vision in the distance, an army of angels. He called that place Mahanaim, meaning "God's army."

Concerned, Jacob sent messengers to Esau asking for forgiveness and that they let bygones be bygones. The messengers returned, telling Jacob that Esau was marching to meet Jacob with a four hundred man army. This scared Jacob even more. Afraid of Esau's vengeance, Jacob sent ahead rich gifts for his brother and his marauding army: two hundred she-goats, twenty he-goats, ewes, rams and camels—all in large quantities, to suit even a king of the desert.

Worried about his brother's reception, Jacob was unable to sleep and left the camp to spend some time alone in prayer. He was pacing on top of the hill when a stranger stopped him and began to wrestle with him. They both struggled in silent duel through the night and into the dawn. Jacob's thigh was sprained but he continued to grapple until the stranger, realizing that he could not prevail, asked Jacob to release him.

"Not until you bless me," Jacob said, sensing that he could not be a mortal.

"What is your name?" asked the stranger.

"Jacob."

"From now on your name will be Israel." And the stranger blessed Jacob.

"And what is your name?" called Jacob. But, before he received an answer, the stranger was gone.

Jacob was deeply touched. "I have seen God face to face and yet I live," he gasped, exhausted yet strangely strengthened. After that night Jacob was a different person. A transformation took place in him in this second revelation of God.

He named that place Peniel, meaning " the face of God."

On his way back to camp after sunrise Jacob saw Esau and his four hundred men approaching his camp. Limping on one leg, he went to meet his brother. After wrestling with the supernatural all night, Jacob had renewed courage.

Having not seen his brother for two decades, Jacob bowed low in front of him seven times. The brothers embraced. Esau declared that he had long ago forgiven all of Jacob's offenses. There was a great deal to talk about, many things had happened in twenty years. Jacob wanted to know how his mother Rebekah and father Isaac were. Esau related that Rebekah had died many years ago and how Isaac, now completely blind and feeble but still alive, always talked about his wife Rebekah and son Jacob.

12. Dinah

The reunited brothers feasted for several days. Then the caravan started to trudge on again. From Haran to Canaan it was about five hundred miles. Traveling with a large herd and several small children meant slow progress. After every few miles they had to find water and take a long rest. It took not only months, but years, to make the long journey.

At one stop something happened which Jacob could neither forget nor forgive his sons. Peace with Esau was still a very tender spot and required tactful courtesy. They were crossing land inhabited by different tribes. Jacob was well aware how cautious they had to be so as not to provoke an attack by them. But his youthful sons paid no heed.

By now Leah's daughter Dinah was a beauty of sixteen or seventeen. While the caravan camped for a longer than usual time, Dinah went on a visit with her relatives. There, while strolling with her friends and servants, she met a rich young man, Shechem, the prince of the Hivites. He liked Dinah and, seducing her, brought the young Hebrew girl to his father's house to marry her.

Hearing about this, Jacob's sons became very indignant. All they wanted was retaliation. Shechem and his father Hamor tried to appease the enraged brothers by telling them that their intentions were honest. After many talks and an exchange of gifts, Jacob made peace with Hamor.

Shechem, who loved Dinah, wanted to make peace with her brothers also.

"Let me find favor in your eyes," he implored the angry brothers. "Whatever you ask of me, I will do."

Jacob's sons held a conference. After that they said deceitfully to Shechem, "We can not give our sister in marriage until you and all your menfolk become just like us—circumcised!"

Shechem was willing to be circumcised. He could speak for himself. But it was an entirely different matter when it came to speaking for all the other males of his tribe. How could he persuade them to have this seemingly unreasonable surgery performed? His love for Dinah was great enough, and he convinced all his men to be circumcized.

On the third day, after numerous operations were performed and when the men were sore and running high fevers, Jacob's sons attacked the Hivites. They slew Hamor, his son Shechem and every male of the tribe. They took Dinah by force from the house of Shechem and, along with her all the loot.

When Jacob heard about the savage reprisal he was greatly distressed.

"Should we treat our sister as a harlot?" retorted his sons self-righteously.

Dinah grieved for her bridegroom a long time, for she loved Shechem, his gentleness and generosity.

Jacob could never forgive his sons, especially Simeon and Levi, leaders of the cruel massacre.

In fear of God's punishment and the vengeance of neighboring tribes, Jacob with the entire household fled to the holy place, Bethel. There he built an altar and put himself to prayer, knowing that God was with him.

Rachel was pregnant with her second child. It was a difficult pregnancy as she was sick most of the time. The hardships of the road added to her suffering. They left Bethel and were on the way to Ephrath when she travailed in great pain. Nothing could help her, not all the skills of the midwives or even the great tenderness and love of Jacob. As soon as the midwife announced the news of gladness about the newborn son, Rachel uttered her last words, "His name is Benoni," which means "son of my sorrow." Whereupon, Rachel's soul departed her.

When Jacob heard it, although in deepest bereavement, he contradicted his wife's final wish. Is it not the father of the son who is entitled to give him a name? And he called his newborn Benjamin, which means "son of the right hand" or "son of the South."

Jacob buried his beloved wife Rachel on the way to Ephrath, later called Bethlehem. There he erected a tomb for her which still stands and is visited by numerous pilgrims.

How cold and empty Jacob's life was since Rachel had died. It was a very sad journey for him and, deeply depressed, he came to Mamre, near Hebron, to his father Isaac's house. Isaac was now one hundred and eighty. It seemed that all these years the Lord had kept him alive to see the reconciliation between his two sons.

Esau and Jacob, now in advanced age, stood side by side at their father's deathbed. Isaac died in peace and his two sons buried him in the family tomb on the land which Abraham bought from a Hittite, in the cave of Macpelah.

Esau, after the mourning period was over, took his wives, children and entire household and left for the hill country of Seir, making Jacob the only heir to his father's inheritance.

13. Joseph — the Beloved Son

Jacob's life in Canaan, with Rachel and his father now gone, would have been quite empty if it were not for Joseph. Benjamin, still a baby, was given to the wet-nurse's care. Jacob loved Joseph, now a teenager, more than any of his other sons.

Now Jacob had twelve sons: six from Leah whose names were Reuben, the first born, Simeon, Levi, Judah, Issachar and Zebulun; two sons from Rachel's maid Bilah, Dan and Naphtali; from Leah's maid Zilpah came Asher and Gad; and, Joseph and Benjamin from Rachel.

Joseph's character was very much like his grandfather Isaac's kind, affectionate, honest and sincere. He was agile in body and mind, surpassing all of his brothers in intelligence. Joseph had Rachel's eyes and her oval-shaped face. Jacob enjoyed his company, keeping the boy always near him and lavishing him with gifts and affection. For Jacob, Joseph was a living symbol of his love for his beloved Rachel.

Jacob's constant attention and preference toward one son caused envy in his other sons. As Joseph grew up into a handsome lad, so grew the brothers' jealousy.

For Joseph's seventeenth birthday present, Israel made him a new robe with long sleeves and many bright colors, like that of a nobleman. When the brothers saw him coming to the field in his new coat, they hated him even more. Weren't they working hard enough to deserve better treatment? Why all this fuss about the boy who was neither a shepherd nor a plowman? All he did was waste his time in the company of the old man, too lazy to work, the agitated brothers complained to each other.

Joseph, approaching them from the hill, greeted his brothers in joyous innocence, eager to share the dream he had had last night.

"Behold," he said gaily, "I had a dream. We were binding

sheaves and my sheaf arose and stood upright. Your sheaves gathered around it and bowed down to my sheaf."

"Are you going to reign over us?" they asked angrily.

But that wasn't all. He had another dream and recalled that one also: the sun, the moon and the eleven stars were bowing down to him

When Jacob heard this he rebuked Joseph, "Shall I, your mother and your brothers indeed come to bow ourselves before you?"

The brothers were enraged, but Jacob kept the words in mind.

One day Jacob asked Joseph to go to the distant pasture at Dothan where his brothers were herding sheep and cattle. "See if all goes well with your brothers and flock and bring me word again."

Gaily singing in his youthful exuberance, Joseph strolled to meet his brothers. Hearing him approach from a great distance, they conspired against him.

"Let's put an end to all this nonsense," suggested one.

"Let's kill him! That is the only way to stop the injustice done to us!" said another.

Reuben, the eldest son who held natural authority over the brothers, objected to the plan. "Shed no blood," he said. "Lay him into this pit here in the wilderness."

The pit was a dried up well, deep and dark. Reuben, not wanting to see the cruelty of his brothers, moved on with his flock before Joseph arrived.

"At sundown I'll come and rescue my younger brother," thought Reuben on his way to a different pasture.

When Joseph was within hearing distance they called, "Here comes the dreamer who wants to rule us. Let us see how true his dreams are!" With that, they stripped off his new robe and cast him into the deep pit.

Joseph cried for mercy, but the brothers just laughed at him. They moved a short distance away from the pit and sat down to have their lunch.

In the afternoon the brothers saw a caravan from Damascus passing by. Soon they learned that these were Ishmaelites on their way to Egypt. Upon seeing the merchants, Judah suggested, "Why not sell Joseph instead of leaving him to die in a pit without making any profit?" The brothers agreed.

They quickly got long ropes and lowered them into the well. "We just wanted to scare you," they called into the well. "Hold on to the ropes and we will pull you out."

After they pulled Joseph out of the darkness, they immediately bound him with the same ropes and sold him to the merchants for twenty silver shekels. The Ishmaelites, afraid that he might run away, harnessed Joseph to a camel before setting out on the long journey over the hot desert sand to Egypt.

Just before the day's end, Reuben returned to the pit. Finding it empty, he grieved for his brother Joseph. Meantime Israel's sons killed a lamb, tore Joseph's robe into shreds and dipped it into the lamb's blood. When they showed their father the torn bloody shreds, Jacob instantly recognized the robe as the one he had given Joseph on his seventeenth birthday. Thinking that wild beasts had devoured his beloved son, Jacob cried relentlessly.

According to custom, Jacob tore his garments, put on sackcloth and scattered ashes on his head in deep mourning. He never stopped grieving for his beloved son and refused to be consoled.

14. Joseph in Egypt

When the Ishmaelites arrived in Egypt they sold Joseph at the marketplace as a slave to the Egyptian Potiphar, a high-ranking officer of Pharaoh.

It did not take long for Potiphar to realize his new slave's intelligence and talent. He saw Joseph as a trustworthy, able young man, a good manager of people and affairs. In a short while Potiphar entrusted Joseph with a high position in his household.

Potiphar was frequently away from home answering the call

of duty. His lonesome wife noticed the handsome Hebrew slave, young virile and single. She watched him lovingly day after day, making advances. But Joseph did not yield to her.

Then she adorned herself with even greater care and spent more time in Joseph's presence. The young Hebrew noticed it and tried desperately to avoid her, but that aroused her passion even more. One day she caught him by the sleeve and said "Lie with me!"

Joseph was startled.

"How can I commit such a sin against my God?" he asked alarmed. "My master has entrusted me with everything in his house except yourself, because you are his wife. How can I betray his trust?"

"Lie with me!" insisted Potiphar's impassioned wife, embracing Joseph. Joseph pulled himself out of her grip. As he was turning to leave the room, she grabbed his cloak. Joseph left his cloak in her hands and hurriedly left her presence.

Potiphar's wife was filled with indignation. It was a humiliation and insult to her womanhood. She decided to revenge herself and her shame.

When Potiphar returned she showed him Jacob's fine cloak, saying, "Your Hebrew servant came in to me and insulted me, but when I called for help, he fled the house, leaving his cloak behind."

Potiphar felt sad because never had his affairs gone so well, as under Joseph's management. But there was no other recourse than to arrest and imprison Joseph.

The prison's chief guard noticed that Joseph was not merely a common criminal. He was kind and polite to everyone, and knew the answers to many complicated problems. He was liked by all, even the rowdiest prisoners. Before long they listened to Joseph, respected him and even asked for his opinion.

One morning two prisoners accused of attempting to poison the Pharaoh awoke from disturbing dreams. One was Pharaoh's butler, the other his chief baker.

The butler told his dream to Joseph and asked him to interpret it. In his dream the butler saw a vine with three branches. The branches budded and blossomed and soon were covered with clusters of ripe grapes. The butler dreamed he had made wine from these grapes and gave it in a cup to Pharaoh to drink.

Joseph said to the butler, "Within three days Pharaoh will free you and restore you to your old position. Remember me to Pharaoh when things go well with you."

The butler assured Joseph he would do all within his might. But when he was released in three days, just as Joseph predicted, the butler forgot about his promise.

Hearing such a positive interpretation of a dream, the chief baker hastily related his own to Joseph.

"I also had a dream," recounted the baker. "There were three cake baskets on my head. The birds were eating from the upper basket containing all sorts of baked goods for the Pharaoh."

"Within three days," Joseph said, Pharaoh will lift up your head from you and hang you on a tree, and the birds will eat your flesh."

Things happened exactly as Joseph predicted.

Joseph spent two more years in prison, until Pharaoh himself had a chain of dreams which disturbed his rest night after night. He called all his chiefs, priests and magicians to the palace to help explain the meaning of his dreams, but there was not one person who could understand them.

Then the chief butler remembered Joseph and how true his interpretation of his dreams were. He mentioned it to Pharaoh and immediately Joseph was brought to the palace.

Joseph, shaven and in new clothes, stood before the throne of Pharaoh. The King of Egypt said,

"There is no one who can interpret my dream and I want to see if you can explain its meaning."

"It is not in me. God will give Pharaoh a favorable answer," replied Joseph, who was faithful to one God and not dependent on his own strength or wisdom, but trusting in God alone.

Pharaoh related his dream to Joseph: Pharaoh stood by the banks of the Nile River, out of which came seven fat cows who ate the reed grass; then, out came seven lean cows who ate the fat ones.

The same night he had another dream: Seven ears of grain, plump and tender were growing on a stalk; after them, seven more sprouted, thin and blighted by the east wind; then, the thin ears swallowed up the plump ones.

Joseph was able to interpret Pharaoh's prophetic dreams:

"God has revealed to Pharaoh that there will be seven years of good harvest, followed by seven years of famine. God has shown Pharaoh what to do." Joseph further explained to the ruler of Egypt how to store the food from the surplus of the rich years to suffice for the future lean years.

Pharaoh was so pleased with Joseph's interpretations that he made him overseer of all the land of Egypt. He gave Joseph a large house, servants and chariots. Then he took his signet ring from his own finger and slipped it on Joseph's, to be used as a state seal. He arrayed him in beautiful garments and called him Zaphenath-paneah, meaning "savior of the land" in the Egyptian language.

As for a wife, Pharaoh gave Joseph Asenath, the daughter of the priest of On. Joseph's misfortunes turned into his good. Pharaoh was well-pleased with his service and gave Joseph great power over the land and its people.

The following seven years were rich in harvest and the people did not know what to do with the grain surplus. Joseph bought grain from farmers and stored it in large granaries and elevators. Many laughed at his efforts because they could not believe that such productive soil would one day be barren.

But it happened. After seven fruitful years the Nile did not flood the fields, leaving the fertile deposit on top of the desert sand which is necessary to produce wheat. Before long the unprepared farmers ran out of food. City stores were empty. Throngs of hungry people flocked to Pharaoh's storage houses to buy grain. Joseph had stocked enough grain to sell to all Egyptians. Then the drought spread to other countries and, with it, famine. People came to Egypt from all over to buy grain for themselves and their flocks.

The famine spread to Canaan also. The caravans passing by from Egypt carried grain and rumors that in the land of Goshen the store-houses were filled with food and that there lived a magician who produced grain in the large granaries.

"What are you waiting for?" asked Jacob of his son. "Go to Egypt before we and our flocks perish!"

He sent them all on their way, except Benjamin, too young still for such a long and arduous trip.

Joseph, supervising the sale of the grain, saw the Canaanites and immediately recognized his brothers. He counted them—where was Benjamin?

"Benjamin should be the same age now that I was when they threw me into the pit and sold me to the Ishmaelites," thought Joseph. "Did they do with him as they did with me?" Joseph decided to find out.

When it was Jacob's sons' turn to buy grain, Joseph started to question them through an interpreter, for he did not want them to know who he was.

"Where do you come from?" he asked sternly.

Bowing lowly to Joseph, the ten brothers answered, "From the land of Canaan, our lord, to buy food."

Joseph remembered the dreams of long ago, how the sheaves bowed before him. He said harshly, "You are spies, you have come to see the weakness of the land."

"No, my lord, to buy food have your servants come," they replied. "We are all sons of one man. We are honest men. We are twelve brothers of one man; behold the youngest is this day with his father and one is no more."

"Now I can see you are spies," said Joseph. "By this you shall be tested: you shall not go from this place unless your youngest brother comes here. Send one of you and let him bring your brother."

He put them all in prison for three days. After three days the brothers were brought before Joseph again.

"I fear God," he said to his brothers. "If you are honest men let one of you remain here and the rest of you carry grain for your household and bring your youngest brother to me."

A commotion arose among the brothers. Thinking Joseph did not understand Hebrew, they talked out their affairs right in front of him. Their guilty consciences, all these years buried, were suddenly reawakened.

"Did I not tell you not to sin against the lad?" Reuben reproached them. "Now there comes a reckoning for his blood."

Hearing this, Joseph turned away from his brothers and wept. Then he told the guards to bind Simeon and to take him to prison. To the rest he sold grain, as much as they wanted. When their sacks were filled Joseph gave a secret order to his guards, telling them to return the money into the mouths of their sacks.

Jacob, with Benjamin supporting him, was waiting by the roadside for the return of his sons. He saw right away that Simeon was missing and asked what happened to him. The brothers related the whole story and that the master of the granaries now wanted Benjamin to be brought to him and that Simeon was being held hostage until their return. When Jacob heard this he wailed in grief and said he would never let Benjamin go. Was it not enough that Joseph had been taken away from him? And now Benjamin, his only joy and consolation in old age—never, never!

As the brothers opened their sacks one by one, they found money in each of them, the exact amount which they had paid for the grain.

"What is this that God has done to us?" they asked each other frightened.

The grain soon was eaten, but the famine still prevailed. There was no recourse but to go back to Egypt to buy more food.

Jacob still would not hear of Benjamin going with his brothers.

"Should we all die from hunger?" they wondered among themselves.

Judah, taking courage, went to his father Jacob, now called Israel. "Send the lad with me that we may live and not die. I guarantee his safety. If I do not bring him back to you, then let me bear the blame forever."

His heart aching, Israel consented that Benjamin go. Before they departed, Israel gave them some choice fruits of the land— balm, myrrh, almonds, pistachio nuts and honeycombs—as presents for the stern Egyptian master.

"Take double the amount of money with you," said Israel to his sons. "Carry back the money that was returned in your sacks, perhaps it was an oversight. May God Almighty grant you mercy before the man, that he may send back your other brother and Benjamin."

When Joseph saw Benjamin, his brother of the same mother, before him, a feeling of love and compassion swelled in his heart. He gave orders for his steward to take the brothers to his own home and to prepare a banquet. The brothers, still not recognizing Joseph, thought another trap was being set for them. Upon entering Joseph's house, they tried to explain that they were not thieves, that the money found in the sacks was brought back and, even more, double the amount. The steward reassured them that he had received the full amount for the grain. Showing the hospitality of the host, Joseph's servants brought water to wash the feet of the Canaanites.

At noon Joseph drove home in his splendid chariot. Seeing him, the brothers bowed down to the ground. Joseph inquired about the health of their father. But, when he saw Benjamin, his heart yearned to embrace him. "God be gracious to you, my son," said Joseph with tears filling his eyes.

Not wanting to show his emotions, Joseph left the room to weep in his chamber. Then rinsing his face with water he returned to his brothers.

The food was served according to Egyptian tradition. Joseph

ate alone at the head table, while the brothers ate at the lower table. It was an abomination for Egyptians to eat at the same table with Hebrews.

After the meal Joseph gave orders to fill each brother's sack with food and to put in each their money, the way it was done the first time. In Benjamin's sack he ordered put his own cup, a rare work of art.

Early in the morning, after a cordial farewell from the unpredictable governor, the brothers were sent away. But as soon as they got out of the city gates the Egyptian guards overtook their caravan. Accused by the soldiers of stealing, the brothers were greatly perturbed.

"Why have you returned evil for good?" asked the captain following Joseph's instructions. "Why have you stolen our master's silver cup?"

The brothers swore they had not done such a thing. Hadn't they brought money back which they had found in their sacks?

"With whomsoever of your servants it be found, let him die and the rest of us will be your master's slaves."

The soldiers searched every man's sack, starting with the oldest down to the youngest. Out came money and the silver cup from Benjamin's sack. There was no other alternative but to re-tie the sacks, load them back on the asses and return to the city.

Joseph was waiting for them in his home. As soon as the brothers entered, they fell to the ground.

"What deed is this that you have done?" demanded Joseph sternly.

"What shall we say to my lord?" said Judah, taking the initiative. "God has found out the guilt of your servants. Now we are the slaves of my lord."

"Only the man in whose hand the cup was found shall be my slave. The rest of you may go in peace to your father," Joseph specified.

Judah tried to explain to this severe Egyptian lord what Benjamin meant to their father—that if the boy was not returned, it would be the end of the old man.

"Take me as your slave," Judah pleaded, "and let the lad return to his father."

Hearing that, Joseph could no longer contain himself. He stepped down from his platform and, opening his arms, called to his brothers in Hebrew,

"I am your brother Joseph whom you sold into Egypt! Is my father still alive?"

The brothers were taken aback. It seemed all their wits had suddenly left them. They dared not even breathe. Motionless, they stood there staring at the man who only a few seconds ago was an unyielding Egyptian governor and whose face changed as suddenly as though a mask had fallen from it.

"Come to me, I pray," said Joseph, his voice full of emotion. "Do not be distressed or angry with yourselves. God sent me here to preserve life for you and all the people. Go back to my father and bring him over so that he and you can dwell near me. In the fertile land of Goshen I will provide for you."

And Joseph threw his arms around Benjamin's neck and they both wept, embracing each other.

The past was forgiven and the reconciliation brought peace and happiness into their hearts. Filled with joy and praising the God of their fathers, the eleven sons returned home to their father Israel in Canaan.

"Joseph is still alive! He is ruler over all the land of Egypt," the brothers excitedly exclaimed.

Hearing this, Jacob was stunned. He could not believe it was true. But when they repeated Joseph's words and showed their father the royal gifts sent him by his beloved son, Israel believed.

"That is enough," he assured his sons. "Joseph, my son, is still alive. I will go and see him before I die."

Israel, his eleven sons, their wives and offspring, and the servants, all were busy happily packing for the move to Egypt. By the time everyone was astride camels and asses ready to go, with sheep, goats, cows and fowl trailing behind, they made a long line heading south toward the Nile.

Israel insisted on stopping at Beersheba. There, on the stone of the old altar, he made a sacrifice to the God of Abraham and Isaac. That night God spoke again to Israel in a vision.

"Do not be afraid to go to Egypt," said the well-known Voice, "for I will there make of you a great nation. I will go down with you to Egypt and I will also bring you up again; and Joseph's hand shall close your eyes."

Joseph went in his chariot to meet Israel at the gates of the city. Both father and son wept on each other's shoulders for a long while.

"Now let me die since I have seen your face and know you are still alive," said Israel in ecstasy upon seeing his beloved son for whom he mourned more than fifteen years.

Israel lived in Egypt for many more years. His twelve sons became the foundation of the twelve tribes of Israel whose posterity and possessions in Egypt greatly multiplied.

When Israel was one hundred and forty-seven years old he knew that the remaining days of his life were few. He called Joseph to his bedside. There he made him swear that they would bury him with his fathers, Abraham and Isaac, in the cave of Macpelah. Then Jacob blessed Joseph's two sons, Ephraim and Manasseh. Ephraim was the younger son and Joseph pointed this out to Israel, thinking that his aged father whose eyes were failing had made a mistake by not giving the principal blessing to the eldest to whom, according to his birthright, it belonged. But Israel insisted on blessing the younger son. In years to come it proved that Israel was right, the leader of his people became Ephraim and not Manasseh.

On his last day Jacob summoned to his deathbed all his sons and bestowed his paternal blessings on each of them, according to their due.

Simeon and Levi be cursed for their fierce anger, wrath and cruelty.

"Judah, the lion, will have the sceptre of a ruler . . ."

"Joseph is a fruitful bough," continued Israel blessing his dearest son, "by God almighty who will bless you with blessings of heaven. . . . blessings of the breasts and of the womb."

"Benjamin is a ravenous wolf, in the morning devouring the prey, and at evening dividing the spoil."

Israel died after living in peace and tranquility in Egypt for seventeen years. Joseph closed his father's eyes, as the Voice had prophesied, and ordered Israel's body to be embalmed just like that of an Egyptian nobleman. Then in a long procession the remains of the old patriarch were carried to the cave of Macpelah, to the land of the Hittites, where he was laid to rest next to Abraham and Sarah, Isaac and Rebekah, and his own first wife Leah.

Joseph reached the age of one hundred and ten. Before he died, he told his brothers,

"I am about to die; but God will visit you and bring you out of this land."

The Egyptians mourned Joseph's death. He was embalmed according to the Egyptian custom and put in a coffin inside one of the pyramids.

According to the Bible, when the Hebrews left Egypt they carried the remains of Joseph with them. There is a possibility that Joseph's mummified body will turn up some day.

Chapter III

The Time of Moses

15. God's Prophet and Chosen Leader

After Joseph's death the Israelites multiplied in Egypt in an astonishingly rapid manner. Three centuries after Joseph's reign the Pharaoh did not know much about the man who once governed Egypt so wisely, or rather, he did not wish to remember. Pharaohs were very knowledgeable men, prepared from earliest childhood to rule their country. They were well-educated and thoroughly versed in the history of their people.

All that Pharaoh Seti I could see was a multitude of Hebrews who preserved their identity and did not mix with Egyptians. These Hebrews were foreigners in the land. Since they kept increasing in population faster than the Egyptians, Pharaoh became seriously concerned.

"Behold, the people of Israel are too many and too mighty for us."

He was afraid that in the event of war the Hebrews would join the enemy and attack the Egyptians from within. Hebrews were a threat to the country, and Pharaoh decided to deal harshly with them.

Egyptians were in dread of the people of Israel. So they made the people of Israel serve with rigor, and made their lives bitter with hard service, in mortar and brick, and in all kinds of work in the field."

But the harder people worked, the poorer they became and the faster they multiplied. Then Pharaoh commanded, "Every son that is born to the Hebrews you shall cast into the Nile, but you shall let every daughter live."

Just after the cruel law had been proclaimed, a boy was born to a humble couple from the house of Levi. This couple already had a daughter, Miriam, and another son, Aaron.

The newborn boy looked so full of health and vigor that the mother did not have the heart to destroy him in accordance with the new law. Instead, she kept him secretly for three months.

When she could not safely hide him any longer, she weaved a basket of reeds and coated it with bitumen and pitch to make it waterproof. She placed the infant in the basket and left it among the reeds at the river's edge.

The following morning Bithia, daughter of Pharaoh, with her lady maids and companions went to the river to bathe. When she saw the basket floating among the reeds, Bithia told one of her maids to pull it out of the water. Upon opening the basket they saw a crying baby. Pharaoh's daughter took compassion on the deserted husky Hebrew boy.

When the Egyptian princess was ready to take the foundling home, the Hebrew boy's sister Miriam who was hiding in the bushes watching approached the princess saying, "Shall I go and call the Hebrew woman to nurse the babe?"

"Go!" said the princess. Miriam hurried home and summoned her mother.

When the boy's mother arrived, the princess said to her, "Take this child and nurse him for me, and I will give you wages."

The woman took the child and nursed him. When he was a little boy his mother taught him the Hebrew religion, explaining about Abraham and Jacob. She told him about God's two promises to the patriarchs, that they were the fathers of a great nation and that the Savior would be a descendant of theirs. All these things were carefully taught to the young child.

Then one day Pharaoh's sister sent for the boy. He was brought to the Pharaoh's court as the adopted son of Pharaoh's daughter, Bithia. She called him Moses, "because he was found in the reeds of the river."

Moses received a different kind of education in Pharaoh's palace. He was instructed by priests in the temples about Egyptian hieroglyphic writings, astronomy, engineering and the numerous Egyptian deities. Nevertheless, Moses remained true to the earlier teachings of his mother and, in his heart, worshipped only one God, the God of Abraham.

One day Moses, already a grown man, was on his daily inspection tour of the site where the Hebrews were building a new pyramid for the king. During the course of his tour Moses saw an Egyptian beating a Hebrew. The blood of his forefather Levi rushed into his head, and enraged, he slew the Egyptian. He dug a shallow hole and placed the Egyptian in it, covering the body with sand.

The next day, while walking alone, Moses saw two Hebrews fighting with one another.

"Isn't it enough that my people are so mistreated by their oppressors?" he thought. "Should they fight among themselves, too?"

"Why do you strike your fellow?" Moses asked the man who did the wrong.

Seeing the Egyptian nobleman interfere, the man became indignant, "Who made you a prince and a judge over us? Do you mean to kill me as you killed the Egyptian?"

Moses then realized that his own crime had been observed. Before long Pharaoh, too, knew about the killing and wanted to punish Moses with the death sentence. With the help of his Egyptian mother, Bithia, Moses planned an escape.

There was just one place to go—the desert. Moses left for the wilderness.

Hungry and thirsty, Moses had all but run out of strength when at last he found a well in the Midian Desert. After quenching his thirst, he lay down in the shade of the well and fell asleep.

He was awakened by the noise of women's voices and the bleating of sheep. Before the girls with their father's flock reached the well, shepherds approached from the other side of the hill and tried to get to the well first. Moses watched the scuffle between the young girls and the shepherds. Jumping to his feet, he drove away the shepherds and helped the girls draw water from the well and fill the troughs for their flock.

In a gay mood the girls returned to their father.

"How come you are back so soon today?" asked their father, the priest of Midian.

His seven daughters told him that an Egyptian helped them draw water and, even more, that he delivered them from the hands of the neighboring hostile shepherds.

"And where is he?" asked Jethro, their father. "Why have you left the man? Call him that he may eat bread."

Moses was brought to the Median priest. He remained with the friendly family and, before long, married Zipporah, the oldest daughter. Together they had two sons.

Forty years passed. Moses was content with his life. The beauty of the mountains and peaceful valleys soothed the pain in his heart caused by the thought of his people's fate.

Meanwhile in Egypt, the burden of the Israelites became even heavier. God heard the constant groaning of the Hebrews, enslaved by Egyptians. The time was ripe for the Israelites to be delivered from their oppressors. All that was needed was a leader to guide them away from Egypt into the land promised so long ago to Abraham, Isaac and Jacob.

Moses was tending his flock at the foot of Mount Sinai. The mountain seemed strangely restless. Moses looked at it and wondered what it could be — an approaching storm, an earthquake? One of his lambs climbed higher. He got it down. Then a goat seemed to be bleating so he climbed a few more steps.

There on the side of the mountain, Moses saw a bush all afire. Had lightning hit it? He had not seen any. Regardless, fire in the desert wilderness would terrify anyone; it always means destruction and disaster. His first impulse was to extinguish the fire in order to save the life-giving plants.

Upon closer observation he saw that, although the flames

were very bright, the bush was not actually burning and that all the twigs and leaves were intact. Surprised, he wanted to see what was happening. As soon as he took the first step toward the bush, he heard a voice calling from the bush,

"Moses! Moses!"

"Here I am," replied Moses.

"Do not come near," the voice said. "Put off your shoes from your feet, for the place on which you are standing is holy ground.

"I am the God of your father Abraham, Isaac and Jacob."

Terrified, Moses fell on the ground and hid his face, afraid to look at God.

The Lord told Moses about the sufferings of his people in Egypt and that he was chosen to deliver them from their oppressors.

Forty years is a long enough time to forget and to change, and Moses had done just that. He no longer considered himself a nobleman of Egyptian upbringing, rather a simple shepherd. Besides, he was afraid of Pharaoh. Didn't the Lord know that Pharaoh had sentenced him to death?

"Who am I that I should go to Pharaoh, and bring the sons of Israel out of Egypt?" asked Moses, humble and perplexed.

Thoughts flashed through his head like lightning. Couldn't God choose someone else? Why himself, completely unworthy and unsuited for the awesome task?

God, who knows everything and reads every thought before it even reaches our understanding, saw the turmoil in Moses' head.

"I will be with you," reassured the Voice of God.

Even though slow in speech, Moses was quick in thought. Now he recalled the two scuffling Israelites who rejected him by asking, "Who made you the ruler and the judge?" Would they not reject him once again?

"If I go to the Israelites and say, 'God of your fathers has sent me to you.' they will ask me, 'What is his name?' and what shall I say to them?"

"I AM WHO AM," God said to Moses. He continued, "Say

this to the people of Israel, 'THE LORD,* the God of your fathers, the God of Abraham, the God of Isaac, and the God of
Jacob, has sent me to you."

"Behold, they will not believe me and will say, 'The Lord did
not appear to you.' "

What is it that you have in your hand?" asked the LORD.

"A rod."

"Cast it on the ground," the LORD ordered. Moses threw his
shepherd staff on the ground and it became a serpent. Seeing this,
Moses fled from it. But the LORD said to Moses, "Take it by the
tail."

When Moses caught the serpent by the tail it turned back
into a rod.

Then the LORD said, "Put your hand into your bosom."
Moses did it, but when he took his arm out, to his horror, he saw
that his hand was covered with leprosy.

"Put your hand back in your bosom," said the LORD. Moses
did, and when he pulled it out his hand was as before. All the
discoloration and deformity caused by leprosy had disappeared.

"If they will not believe the first sign, they will heed the second," said the LORD.

"Oh, my Lord," objected Moses, "I am not eloquent. Rather,
I am slow of speech and tongue. I pray, send some other person."

Now the LORD grew impatient with so many objections and
excuses from Moses.

"Am I not the LORD of speech?" the LORD reproached
Moses. "I will send your brother Aaron, the Levite, to meet you.
He can speak well."

With this heavy load upon his mind, Moses went to his father-
in-law and said, "Let me go back to my kinsmen in Egypt and see
whether they are still alive."

Jethro, now an old priest, read in Moses' face and entire bear-

---

*The word LORD when spelled with capital letters, stands for the
divine name,YHWH. **The Holy Bible,** Revised Standard Version. The
Catholic Truth Society, Publishers of the Holy See, London, ©1966.

ing the urgency of his request. "Go," he replied without hesitation. Moses began preparations for the long journey with his wife and two sons. The LORD, seeing that Moses was exceedingly sad and frightened, consoled Moses, "Go back to Egypt; for all the men who were seeking your life are dead."

With the rod of God in one hand, Moses led the ass on which his wife sat with his other hand. They were followed by two more asses carrying their young sons. Thus, Moses set out with his family to the land of Egypt.

Meanwhile, the Lord appeared in a dream to Aaron, bidding him to go into the wilderness to meet Moses. About forty years had passed since they had last seen one another. When the two brothers met, they embraced and kissed each other fondly. Then Moses told Aaron all that God had said to him.

When they arrived in Goshen, Aaron gathered the people of Israel together for a meeting. Moses introduced Aaron who, in turn, spoke to the crowd.

When the people of Israel saw the miracle of the rod and how the leprosy appeared and disappeared on Moses' command, they believed. Bowing their heads, they thanked God for sending them a deliverer.

The following day Moses and Aaron went to Pharaoh and said, "Thus says the LORD, the God of Israel, 'Let my people go.'"

"I do not know the God of Israel. Why should I let your people go?" answered Pharaoh.

Moses showed the miracles of the rod and leprosy, but Pharaoh was not the least bit impressed. His heart was hardened, and he did not want his slaves to go.

God sent one pestilence after another upon the Egyptians, but Pharaoh's heart became even more hardened. Still, he did not listen to Moses and Aaron. On the contrary, he made the yoke of the Hebrews even more burdensome. The Israelites groaned under the heavy burdens and murmured against Moses. Since he had come to Egypt, more evil was wrought upon them and their lives became much more difficult than before.

Many times Moses went to Pharaoh, asking him to release his people. But Pharaoh would not listen. God sent ten horrible plagues upon Egypt. Pharaoh's heart remained hardened.

"Pharaoh will not listen to you," the LORD said to Moses, "that my wonders may be multiplied in the land of Egypt."

Moses again went to Pharaoh and said, "thus says the LORD: 'About midnight I will go forth in the midst of Egypt; and all the first-born in the land of Egypt shall die, from the first-born of the Pharaoh to the first-born of the maid-servant, and all the first-born of the cattle.' "

But still Pharaoh would not heed the words of Moses, and God instructed Moses on how to prepare for this last and most horrible plague, the beginning of the passover.

The Israelites had to take lambs without blemish and kill one for each household. Some of its blood had to be put on each house's doorposts. Then they had to roast and eat the lamb, accompanied with unleaven bread and bitter herbs.

"This is the LORD'S passover," said the Lord, "for I will pass through the land of Egypt that night, and I will smite all the first-born."

When what the Lord had said happened, there was crying and mourning in the land of Egypt as was never before. Stricken by the powerful hand of God and mourning for his own first-born son, Pharaoh told the Israelites to go.

16. A Long Journey

The Israelites had lived in Egypt four hundred and thirty years. When they left the land they were six hundred thousand men on foot, besides women and children.

God did not lead the Hebrews by the shortest route through the land of the Philistines, but by way of the wilderness toward the Red Sea. The Lord went before them by day in a pillar of cloud and by night in a pillar of fire, giving light to them.

After a long march the people encamped between Migdol and the sea. Pharaoh's messengers followed the Israelites and sent back reports as to their progress. When Pharaoh heard that the people were camping between the wilderness and the sea, he knew that they were trapped. Immediately he ordered his Egyptian army and chariots to pursue them and attack, driving the Hebrews into the sea.

All this was in God's plan so that he might show his majesty and care for his people, the Hebrews.

As the Egyptians approached, panic arose among the Israelites.

"Lift up your rod," the Lord told Moses, "and stretch out your hand over the sea and divide it, that the people of Israel may go on dry ground through the sea."

Moses did as God commanded. He stretched his hand with the rod in it, and the east wind blew, making a division in the sea with dry ground in the middle. The people of Israel went into the midst of the sea on the dry ground. The Egyptians pursued them into the Red Sea.

When the last Israelite reached the sea's far shore, the Lord said to Moses, "Stretch out your hand over the sea, that the water may come back upon the Egyptians."

Moses did just that. The waters returned and covered the Egyptian army and their chariots.

The people of Israel continued on their way, praising the Lord for saving them with the might of his hand. They sang a new song to the Lord who had triumphed so gloriously over their enemies.

Moses began the song and the people echoed after him:

"I will sing to the LORD, for he has triumphed gloriously;
    the horse and his rider he has thrown into the sea.
The Lord is my strength and my song,
    and he has become my salvation;
    this is my God, and I will praise him,
    my father's God, and I will exalt him. . . ."

Miriam, Aaron's sister, took a tambourine in her hands and, singing with the other women, began dancing. The others joined in and the Hebrews rejoiced over their exodus from Egypt.

"Thou hast led in thy steadfast love the people whom thou hast redeemed, thou hast guided them by thy strength to thy holy abode. . . ."

The jubilant people sang, repeating one verse many many times:

"THE LORD WILL REIGN FOR EVER AND EVER."

The Israelites moved on through the desert into the wilderness of Shur. After many tiresome days they came to Lake Marah, but its water was too bitter to drink. The people, thirsty and exhausted, complained against Moses, murmuring, "What shall we drink?"

Moses prayed to the Lord and he showed him a tree. Moses took a branch from it, dipped it into the water and the water became sweet.

They then came to the wilderness of Sin, not far from Mount Sinai. Now they were underway the second month and the food supplies which they had brought from Egypt had run out. The mass of people was hungry and exhausted. When people are hungry they become resentful and dissatisfied.

They complained to Moses and Aaron:

"In Egypt we sat by the fleshpots and ate bread to the full. You have brought us out into this wilderness to kill our whole assembly with hunger."

God heard their dissatisfaction, and told Moses:

"Behold, I will rain bread from heaven for your people in the morning and will give flesh to eat in the evening. Every morning people will collect only one day's portion, but on the sixth day, two days' portion. In the morning you shall see the glory of the LORD, because he has heard your murmuring against the LORD."

"Who am I that you murmur against me?" asked Moses of his assembled people. "It is God the LORD you murmur against. He has heard your murmurings and he will show you that he is the LORD who brought you out of Egypt."

The next morning when the people woke up, they saw dew covering all the plants and the ground. When the morning sun had dried up the dew there were fine flakes on the ground. The people wondered what it was. Moses explained to them that it was bread from heaven, manna, from which each was to gather one day's portion. But there were some who were greedy and gathered more than they could consume in one day. The part that was left for the next day became foul and infested with worms.

The people in the desert had as much bread in the morning as they could eat. When twilight came the Lord sent them quails in such quantity that they covered the camp. Thus, the people had enough meat for supper.

Moses told Aaron to take a jar, put an omer* of manna in it, and place it before the Lord, to be kept throughout the generations. This "Bread of Heaven" was a strikingly prophetic sign of the Holy Eucharist kept in the tabernacles of our churches today.

The Israelites ate manna for forty years, throughout their wanderings in the desert, until they came to the borders of the Promised Land.

Moving southward, the Hebrews came to Rephidim. After encampment they discovered that no water was to be found. Their skins and barrels were empty. The people complained to Moses, "Give us water to drink."

Moses was perplexed. When would his people learn to put their trust in the Lord?

"Why do you find fault with me?" he asked his people. "Why do you put the Lord to the proof?"

But the people murmured against Moses, forgetting all the past blessings the Lord had given them, saying, "Why did you bring us up from Egypt to kill us and our children with thirst?"

Moses prayed to the Lord, and the Lord told him to strike the rock of Mount Horeb with his rod. Moses gathered the elders

---

*Omer — an ancient Hebrew dry measure equal to about 3.7 quarts.

around the rock and smote it with his rod. Water came out of the side of the rock. First slowly trickling down, the stream became wider and wider until water was gushing like a river from the side of the mountain.

The Israelites encountered another problem in Rephidim. The tribe of Amalek attacked them when they were least suited for fighting. Moses called on Joshua, one of his young brave men and a strong believer. He told him to choose young men for battle.

"Tomorrow," said Moses, "I will stand on top of the hill with the rod of God in my hand."

The battle started early in the morning. Whenever Moses held up his rod, Israel prevailed. Whenever he lowered his hand, Amalek prevailed. The old man's arms grew weary. Aaron and Hur, Miriam's husband, made Moses sit on a stone. They held his arms up, one on each side, until Joshua and his men conquered Amalek and his warriors.

When the people were refreshed after a good rest in Rephidim, Moses told them to break camp. Walking in front of the congregation, he led them further south into the wilderness of Sinai.

They encamped near majestic Mount Sinai. Jethro, the Midian priest and Moses father-in-law, heard about Moses arrival. He took his daughter Zipporah, whom Moses sent back to her father from Egypt, and their two sons to see Moses. It was a very joyous family reunion. Moses told his father-in-law about Pharaoh, the ten plagues and about the exodus from Egypt.

Jethro praised the Lord for delivering the Israelites from the hand of the Pharaoh. Together with Moses, he offered a burnt sacrifice to God.

"Now I know that the Lord is greater than all gods," said the old priest. "Blessed be the Lord."

The next day Jethro watched Moses judge the people. Crowds gathered around Moses from morning until late at night, asking him to help settle their problems and disputes.

Jethro advised Moses to choose able men as judges of the people and that only in important matters should he himself make decisions. Moses heeded the advice of his father-in-law. The new order gave him more time to withdraw from the crowd to talk to the Lord in prayer.

17. The Ten Commandments

The Israelites were encamped at the foot of Mount Sinai. They were in a fertile valley with an abundance of fresh water and green grass. People liked the place and wanted to remain.

Moses, sitting in front of his tent, raised his eyes toward the top of the majestic mountain, remembering his first encounter with God—the burning bush and the Lord's Voice telling him to lead his people out of the bondage of Egyptians. How trustworthy was God! How steadfast in his love! Moses thought about the many miracles God had worked for his people and about his guidance and providence.

Holding his rod in hand, the grey-haired shepherd felt a strange stirring in his heart. The mountain was alive again, just like on that day when he saw the burning bush. Its top was enwrapped by a cloud that did not move away. The mountain seemed to be vibrating.

The first time it was out of curiosity that Moses climbed up to see the burning bush. This time it was a definite urge in Moses' heart to ascend the mountain. Before he realized what he was doing, Moses was working his way up the mysterious mount. In the middle of his climb, a huge eagle wildly flapped its wings over its egg-filled nest as Moses passed by. Then everything happened very quickly—he was on top of the mountain which was still covered by the cloud.

"You have seen what I did to the Egyptians," he heard the familiar voice speak, "and now I bore you on the eagle's wings and brought you to myself. Now therefore, if you will obey my voice and keep my covenant, you shall be my own possession among all peoples; for all the earth is mine, and you shall be to

me a kingdom of priests and a holy nation. These are the words
which you shall speak to the children of Israel."

Full of God's spirit, happy and inspired, not even feeling his
age, Moses hurried down the hill to give the message to his people.
The congregation was standing like an army at attention when
Moses repeated the message, stressing, "You shall be my own
possession . . . a kingdom of priests. . . ." In unison the people
promised, "All that the Lord has spoken we will do."

Up to the top the white-clad Moses climbed again to bring
the promise of his people to the Lord. But the Lord God knew
how the moods of the people change, and he had prepared more
lasting impressions for their minds. He would come in a thick
cloud so that people could see it and would believe their prophet,
Moses.

The Lord told Moses to go down and consecrate his people
to God. They would have to wash their garments, stay away from
sensual pleasures for three days and be prepared for the Lord. On
the third day the Lord God would come down upon Mount Sinai.

"Take heed that you do not go up into the mountain or touch
it," warned the Lord. "Whoever touches the mountain shall be
cut to death. . . . When the trumpet sounds a big blast, they shall
come up to the mountain."

On the third day majestic Mount Sinai was full of life and
power. There was thunder and lightning from the thick cloud
around its summit, and a deafening trumpet blast sounded. "Is this
our end or the end of everything?" wondered the terrified people.
Trembling from fear, people assembled around the base of the
mountain to meet God. Aaron and Hur set boundaries around
the mountain, which seemed to breathe with life. There was no
concern for trespassers, everyone was afraid to go near it.

And Mount Sinai was wrapped in smoke, because the LORD
descended upon it in fire; and the smoke of it went up like the
smoke of a kiln, and the whole mountain quaked greatly."

Many fell on their faces. Many repented their sins. People
not only believed, but they knew that God was indeed on this

mountain. God told Moses to climb the mount and to bring Aaron with him. Moses went down and got Aaron. Both brothers climbed Mount Sinai together. But Aaron did not ascend to the top, he was to wait farther down for Moses.

The Lord God spoke in a powerful voice which the entire trembling congregation heard:

"I am the LORD your God, who brought you out of the land of Egypt, out of the house of bondage.

"You shall have no other gods before me.

"You shall not make for yourself a graven image, or any likeness of anything that is in heaven above, or that is in the earth beneath . . . for I the LORD your God am a jealous God, visiting the iniquity of the fathers upon the children to the third and fourth generation of those who hate me, but showing steadfast love to thousands of those who love me and keep my commandments.

"You shall not take the name of the LORD your God in vain; for the LORD will not hold him guiltless who takes his name in vain.

"Remember the sabbath day, to keep it holy. . . .

"Honor your father and your mother, that your days may be long in the land which the LORD your God gives you.

"You shall not kill.

"You shall not commit adultery.

"You shall not steal.

"You shall not bear false witness against your neighbor.

"You shall not covet your neighbor's house . . . or anything that is your neighbor's."

Seeing and hearing the power of God, the people were completely shaken with fear. They turned to Moses and begged of him, "You speak to us, and we will hear; but let not God speak to us, lest we die."

"Do not fear," said Moses to his people. "God has come to prove you, and that the fear of him may be before your eyes, that you may not sin."

With that, Moses departed from his people and climbed back

to the top of Mount Sinai where God waited in the form of a cloud. There the Lord instructed Moses, explaining the Ten Commandments in detail.

The greatest and most frightening commandment for Israel was the first one—to love God and not to worship idols. To love an unknown and unseen God, while all nations worshipped idols, was very difficult. Many Hebrews brought with them from Egypt household deities, things they could hold, touch and see. There were many superstitions among people. But, there was to be no compromise. God required all or nothing — all their love, pure hearts and absolute possession.

On Mount Sinai the Lord God engraved two stone tablets with the ten most important precepts and gave them to Moses. Moses spent forty days and forty nights on Mount Sinai, taking instruction from the Lord God.

The people in the valley became restless. Why was Moses tarrying so long? The immigrants from Egypt were left like a shepherdless flock. There was no one to guide them. They went astray. Aaron was to take Moses' place while Moses was gone, but he had neither his power nor authority. Besides, people knew too well that Aaron was not going to lead them to the Promised Land. They needed something or someone to guide them. Before long, the quiet whispers of discontent became loud demands:

"Make us gods, who shall go before us. As for this Moses, the man who brought us up out of the land of Egypt, we do not know what has become of him."

From their wives, daughters and sisters, they collected gold jewelry: rings, bracelets, earrings and pins. Melting it all in one mold, they made a golden calf.

Who can understand or attempt to explain why? Even Aaron, Moses' brother and closest associate, when he saw the golden calf, he himself built an altar for it. He made the proclamation:

"Tomorrow shall be a feast to the Lord."

"They arose early the next morning and offered burnt sacrifices and brought peace offerings; and the people sat down to eat and drink, and rose up to play."

The Lord God was aware of his people worshipping the idol and was angry about their corruption. He would have destroyed them with one sweep of his hand, had not Moses interceded for them.

"O Lord," pleaded Moses on top of Mount Sinai, unaware of the disobedience of his people below, "why does thy wrath burn hot against thy people, whom thou hast brought forth out of the land of Egypt with great power and with a mighty hand?"

Moses reminded God of his faithful servants, Abraham, Isaac and Jacob. He told the Lord that the Egyptians would say that the God of Israel had taken them into the desert to be killed. Scripture says: "And the Lord repented of the evil which he thought to do to his people."

When Moses came down the mountain he saw what was going on in the encampment. He could not believe his own eyes! How could his people turn away from God in such a short time? What he saw was horrifying: God's chosen people were singing and dancing around the golden calf in an outright pagan orgy.

Shocked and enraged, Moses did what Christ was to do during his lifetime when he entered the temple of Jerusalem and found profanity in it*: he destroyed the idol and scattered the worshippers.

The Old Testament's description of Moses' feeling is very powerful:

". . . Moses' anger burnt hot, and he threw the tables out of his hands and broke them at the foot of the mountain. And he took the calf which they had made, and burnt it with fire, and ground it to powder, and scattered it upon the water, and made the people of Israel drink it."

So great was the wrath of Moses that, standing in the gate of the camp, he called to his people, "Who is on the Lord's side? Come to me."

---

*Jesus overturned the tables of money-changers and chased them out with a whip of cords saying, "My house shall be called a house of prayer for all the nations, but you have made it a den of robbers." Cf., Jn. 2, 13-15; Mk. 11, 15-17.

All the sons of Levi gathered around him.

"Thus says the LORD God of Israel," shouted the aged prophet with unearthly power in his voice, " 'Put every man his sword on his side, and go to and fro from gate to gate throughout the camp, and slay every man his brother, and every man his neighbor.' "

The sons of Levi did as Moses commanded. There were three thousand men slain that day. Through this blood bath the sons of Levi ordained themselves for the service of God and became his priests.

On the next day Moses returned to Mount Sinai to make atonement for his people. Ashamed and disheartened about the behavior of the Israelites, he asked the Lord to blot him out of the Lord's book.

"Whoever has sinned against me, him I will blot out of my book," responded the Lord. "But now go, lead the people to the place of which I have spoken to you; behold, my angel shall go before you. Nevertheless, in the day when I visit, I will visit their sin upon them."

When the people heard God's message they mourned. They took off their ornaments and repented.

Moses' tent was pitched outside of the camp. People came to his tent to join in prayer. "Has God forsaken us?" they anxiously asked themselves.

Then one day they saw a cloud above Moses' tent. They knew then that God was still with them.

The Lord told Moses to make another set of tablets just like the first ones and to bring them to Mount Sinai. On top of the mountain God inscribed the Ten Commandments on both sides of the tablets.

Moses spent another forty days on top of the mountain without food or water. There the Lord God passed before Moses, but Moses did not see the face of the Lord, only his back. There God proclaimed to Moses his name: "The LORD, a God merciful and gracious, slow to anger, and abounding in steadfast love and faithfulness. . . ."

*Even from a distance, the people noticed
a change in Moses' bearing.*

When Moses came down from Mount Sinai with the two tablets upon which the words of the covenant had been written, the people noticed a change in Moses' bearing and, when he came closer, also in his face. His face shone with brilliant radiance because he had seen and talked with God.

Aaron was in the foreground with the Israelites standing behind him. Upon seeing Moses' face they stepped back. They were afraid to go near Moses because they had never seen such a phenomenon—an unearthly light veiled the man's face.

Moses, not realizing the change in his own countenance, beckoned his people to come closer. Cautiously, they approached him. Not being able to withstand the brilliance emanating from his face, they asked him to cover it. After that Moses walked among his people with his face veiled, and only when in the presence of the Lord, did he remove the veil.*

18. The Tabernacle

That day Moses dismissed his people and told them to reassemble in the morning. When the congregation was ready, Moses addressed them:

"These are the things that the Lord has commanded you to do. Six days shall work be done, but on the seventh day you shall have a holy sabbath of solemn rest to the Lord."

Moses explained how God had commanded him to bring an offering from the people to the Lord of gold, silver, bronze, acacia wood, fine linens and other prized goods, and to make a tabernacle in which the Lord would dwell forever. Hearing that, the people were filled with joy and a sense of great relief. Once again God

---

*An analogy to this, found in the New Testament, is the transfiguration of Jesus Christ on Mount Tabor, when Christ prayed in the presence of Peter, James and John. Cf., Mt. 17, 1-2; Mk. 9, 2-8; and Lk. 9, 28-36.

had forgiven their iniquities. They brought their offerings with willing hearts.

Just as before the great deluge when God gave a detailed plan to Noah on how to build the ark, so again God gave detailed instructions to Moses on how to construct the Ark of the Covenant, the Tabernacle. This was to be a permanent dwelling for the Lord, where the Israelites would have a fixed place of worship.

Their patriarchs had offered sacrifices to God in many different places. The head of the family was the priest. Conversing with God on the mountain, Moses received from the Lord clear directions regarding divine worship.

The most skillful artisans were selected to build this tabernacle or shrine. It was portable and well-suited for the wandering people of Israel. The tabernacle was made of precious acacia wood and consisted of many frames fitted together, so that it could be taken apart and reassembled easily. It was thirty cubits* long, by ten cubits in width and height. The bars for carrying the tabernacle fitted into gold rings. Inside the shrine was the table of acacia wood overlaid with pure gold, with a lampstand of pure gold also. Inside was the altar of incense overlaid with pure gold. The tabernacle had ten curtains of fine linen in blue, purple and scarlet, with cherubim skillfully worked into them.

The tabernacle was divided into two parts: the forepart, which was the larger, was called the sanctuary; the smaller part was called the Holy of Holies. Each part was separated from the other by a curtain.

Upon seeing the completed work, Moses blessed the artisans because they had done exactly as God had commanded.

On the first day of the first month in the second year after the exodus from Egypt, the tabernacle was erected. A tent was placed around it for protection. In the Holy of Holies Moses placed the Ark of the Covenant which was covered inside and out with pure gold. In the Ark he put the tables of law, the Ten Command-

---

*Cubit—an ancient linear measurement equivalent to about 18-22 inches or about 45.7-55.9 centimeters.

ments written by the hand of God. Later on, there was also placed
in the Ark a jar filled with manna and the rod of Aaron.

Only the priests were allowed to enter the Sanctuary; and
into the Holy of Holies, no one but the High Priest could enter
and, then, only once a year on the great day of Expiation.

When all was completed according to God's command, Moses
poured sacred oil on the tabernacle and burned the fragrant incense upon the altar. He then offered the cereal oblation, as the
Lord had instructed him.

When Moses finished the offering, people outside saw the
cloud descending and hovering above the tent. Thus they knew
that the glory of God had filled the Tabernacle. This was the sign
given to the Israelites: whenever the cloud was lifted up from the
Tabernacle, it would be time to move on; whenever the cloud rested above the Tabernacle, they were to stay in that place.

"The cloud of the Lord was upon the tabernacle by day, and
fire was in it by night, in the sight of all the house of Israel."

As soon as the tabernacle was brought to completion and
the Lord dwelled within it, Moses was given a new order: to take
a census of the Israelites. This meant that all the males of twenty
years or more had to be counted. Also, they had to be divided into
tribes. The males of Levi were appointed guardians of the Tabernacle, and the sons of Aaron, the priests. This created a great deal
of discontent among the people. Why was one tribe set apart?
Why this particular arrangement? Were they better than the other
sons, those of Jacob?

"This is the way the Lord wants it," was Moses' reply to his
revolting people.

But the Lord had more in store, and he let it be known
through Moses:

"Say to Aaron and his sons, 'Thus you shall bless the people
of Israel: you shall say to them,

The Lord bless you and keep you:

The Lord make his face shine upon you, and give you peace.'

"So shall they put my name upon the people of Israel, and I
will bless them."

Aaron was made the High Priest and the sons of Aaron, the priests, forever. Their priestly blessing is given in temples and churches throughout the world.

19. Moses' Family Problems

Although Moses, especially in his advanced age, was a meek man, he was not spared from family problems. Nor, was he spared from many rebellions from his own people and from his very own relatives.

In his old age, apparently after the death of Zipporah, Moses "made a contract of marriage" with a dark-skinned Cushite woman from an Ethiopian tribe. She was considered a foreigner by the fair-skinned Israelites, and the family members would not accept her as one of them.

Miriam, Moses' sister with the gift of prophecy, was the first to speak against this marriage. It was the pride within her that spoke when she pronounced the degrading remark:

"Has the Lord indeed spoken only through Moses? Has he not spoken through us also?" she asked with indignation.

Her heart was full of jealousy when she said this to her brother Aaron. Aaron agreed—God had spoken through him also. After all, why should Moses, spokesman for the Lord, be involved with this stranger and bring disgrace on the whole family?

The Lord heard their grumblings and suddenly came to Moses' defense.

"Come out, you three, to the tent of meeting," called the Lord.

The Lord, in a pillar of cloud, stood at the door of the tent and called to Aaron and Miriam:

"With him I speak mouth to mouth, clearly, and not in dark speech; and he beholds the form of the Lord. Why then were you not afraid to speak against my servant Moses?"

The Lord departed, the cloud disappeared. The two brothers and their sister stood speechless. Aaron looked at Miriam. Sudden-

ly his facial expression changed to one of complete shock. He saw
Miriam's face, hand and neck, white as snow—a definite sign of
leprosy.

"Oh, my lord, do not punish us because we have done foolish-
ly," Aaron begged of Moses. Moses, just as surprised as Aaron
about the change in Miriam's skin, knew only one answer—prayer.
In all meekness and sincerity, he prayed to God to heal his sister
Miriam, who stood near him when he was a baby floating among
the reeds of the Nile, who looked after him when he was little. The
Lord, as always, listened to Moses' prayers, but, before healing,
Miriam had to go through purification.

"Let her be shut up outside the camp seven days . . ." are the
words in "The Holy Bible."

After seven days Miriam returned to the camp completely
cured. By this time the cloud above the tabernacle had lifted up,
and the Israelites were breaking camp, preparing to move on into
the wilderness of Paran.

20. On the Threshold of the Promised Land

Moving northward, the Israelites crossed the wilderness of
Paran and settled in a beautiful oasis, Kadesh, which had abundant
springs of water, palm trees providing shelter from the sun as well
as nourishment, and green grazing land for cattle. The people were
content.

The first census which the Lord told Moses to take showed
there were 603,550 men who were over twenty years of age. That
could make quite an impressive army of men, even today.

Canaan, the Promised Land, was not far away. Spirits were
high. People thought it would not take much longer to reach the
"land of milk and honey."

While the people were peacefully encamped and enjoying
their rest, Moses selected twelve young men, one from each tribe.

Among them was the renowned hero, Joshua. They were sent into the Promised Land to explore it.

The men returned from their explorations after "forty days": which, according to Hebrew tradition, means a long period of time. They told the congregation that the land was really flowing with milk and honey. As proof of it they brought huge clusters of grapes, so big and heavy that it took two men to carry one such cluster on their shoulders. They also brought other fruits such as figs and pomegranates.

But, alas, they lamented, the land was populated with the sons of Anak who were giants! All of the inhabitants were tall and strong, and their cities were fortified up to heaven! Only Caleb, from the tribe of Judah, and Joshua did not lose courage. They trusted the Lord and were not frightened.

"Do not be in dread or afraid of them," Moses encouraged his people. "The Lord your God who goes before you will himself fight for you."

But the people lost all their courage, became disheartened and would not trust in God's help. They cried and lamented, wishing they had never left Egypt where they sat by fleshpots and had plentiful supplies of cabbage, onions and garlic to eat. It would be better to die in the wilderness or in Egypt, than in bloody battle with these giant people, where their own children would be prey to these monsters!

Some even suggested choosing a new commander and returning to Egypt. A big riot was erupting among the Israelites.

The Lord looked at his rebellious people, and he became angered.

"Not one of these men, of this evil generation shall see the good land which I swore to give your fathers, except Caleb and Joshua," thundered the voice of God.

"But moreover your little ones, who you said would become prey and who this day have no knowledge of good or evil, shall go in there. To them I shall give the land, and they shall possess it. But as for you, turn and journey into the wilderness . . ." Moses and Aaron fell prostrate on their faces and prayed. During the stay in Kadesh Miriam died, and was buried there. From Kadesh they journeyed to Mount Hor. There the Lord told Moses to bring Aaron and Aaron's son Eleazar to the top of Mount Hor. On the mountain God commanded that the priestly garments of Aaron be stripped and put on his son Eleazar.

Aaron died on top of the mountain. Moses and Eleazar came down and told their people what had happened. The House of Israel wept for Aaron for thirty days.

For "forty years" the Israelites wandered in the desert and wilderness. Whenever the murmurings and rebellion of these stubborn, stiff-necked people threatened to get out of control, the Lord God would send a pestilence upon them as punishment, until they humbled themselves and repented.

One time God punuished his people with serpents whose venomous bite caused many to die.

"We have sinned against the Lord," cried the people in distress.

"Repent, repent . . ." was the warning from Moses. His face buried in the ground, he asked the Lord to take away the punishment. God instructed Moses to make a serpent of brass as a sign of their sin, and to lift it up on a tall pole in the desert, as the future symbol of the crucifix and salvation.* Whomever was bitten and looked upon it was cured.

At last, in the fortieth year of their wanderings the House of Jacob came to the banks of the Jordan River.

"This is the land which I swore to Abraham, to Isaac and to Jacob, saying, 'I will give it to your descendants,' " said the Lord to Moses, showing him the green valley of the Promised Land below. Even Moses was not permitted to enter the Promised Land, and he knew it. His mission was over.

Before his departure, Moses blessed the tribes of Jacob and made a lengthy sermon. It seems there was one thing he wanted

---

*Jesus told Nicodemus: "As Moses lifted up the serpent in the wilderness, so must the Son of man be lifted up, that whoever believes in him may have eternal life." Jn. 2:14-15.

to impress upon the minds and souls of his people, and this was the core of his speech:

"Hear, O Israel: the Lord our God is one Lord; and you shall love the Lord your God with all your heart, and with all your soul, and with all your might. . . . The Lord your God will raise up for you a prophet like me from among you, from your brethren—him you shall heed. . . ."

He foretold to his people that one day another prophet would rise in their midst, who also would institute a covenant, a covenant of salvific love, the New Testament. As God instituted the Old Covenant through Moses, so Jesus would begin the New Covenant.

In his last address to his people, Moses reminded them of all the wonders which God had wrought in their behalf. He promised them that if they were faithful in observing the commandments of the Lord they would be blessed in their houses, in their fields, blessed in the fruits of the land and in everything. Then he warned them, if they did not heed the voice of the Lord and did not keep his commandments, curses would come upon them and all they possessed.

After praying for his people, he blessed every tribe with a special blessing. Then, upon departing, Moses spoke the following canticle of praise:

> *"Give ear, O heavens, and I will speak;*
> *and let the earth hear the words of my mouth.*
> *May my teaching drop as the rain,*
> *my speech distil as the dew,*
> *as the gentle rain upon the tender grass,*
> *and as the showers upon the herb.*
> *For I will proclaim the name of the Lord.*
> *Ascribe greatness to our God!"*

Moses went up from the plains of Moab to Mount Nebo, opposite Jericho. There, once again, the Lord showed him all the Promised Land. Here, too, it was that Moses died.

Scripture says that "his eye was not dim, nor his natural force abated," even though he was one hundred and twenty years old when God took him.

His people mourned him for thirty days. There would never be a prophet greater than Moses, nor one who would have greater faith or such burning zeal for God's honor and so much patience and love for his people.

Chapter IV

The Time of the Judges

(about 1450-1095 B.C.)

21. Joshua

Joshua, chosen by Moses as the new leader, was in full charge when the period of mourning was over. He was a man full of courage, wisdom, God's spirit, and deep faith, with a difficult task confronting him: to cross the Jordan River and lead the Israelites, at last, to the land of milk and honey.

Before his death, Moses laid his hands upon Joshua in front of the congregation, so that people would respect and obey their new leader. The laying of hands upon a person and bestowing of a blessing was not only highly revered by Israelites, but it meant the presence of a special grace and mission to fulfill.

Joshua had a heavy burden upon him. The task was not merely to lead, advise and judge people. Much more was required of Joshua. Israel now needed a commander who could lead them in battle to gain possession of the land.

The Israelites were encamped on the east side of the Dead Sea, on the hills and in the valleys scattered with rocks where, once long ago in the time of Abraham, pitch and stones rained from above and buried the two cities with all their sinful inhabitants.

The new commander, Joshua, was faithful to the Voice of the Lord and followed it with deep commitment.

"Moses my servant is dead," said the Voice one day. "Now therefore arise, go over this Jordan, you and all this people, into the land which I am giving to them. As I was with Moses, so I will be with you; I will not fail you or foresake you. Be strong and courageous."

The faith which Joshua had was sufficient. Immediately he ordered his officers to go through the camp and inform the people to prepare to cross the Jordan into the land God had given them.

Just as a precaution, Joshua sent two men to cross the Jordan and go secretly into the walled city of Jericho to view the strength of the enemy. The two spies managed to get through the city gate and, through God's providence, stopped at the house of harlot Rahab who lived in an apartment built into the wall of the city. Rahab sized up the strangers right away, as well as the purpose of their coming. She quickly decided to use the situation to her own benefit.

She told the two young spies how disheartened the city dwellers were about the rumors of how God had protected the Israelites and how he had dried up the Red Sea for them and drowned the Egyptians. The people of Jericho were well informed about the threat from the wandering multitude, and their hearts were melting away with fear. The two spies were glad to hear that.

As soon as the two strangers entered the city, at a time when every foreigner was suspect, the king of Jericho immediately received the message, "Behold, certain men of Israel have come here tonight to search out the land." The king sent his guards to Rahab to bring the spies to him.

Rahab was a woman of beauty with a rouged face and strongly perfumed, dressed in a brightly colored flowing gown and adorned with jingling jewelry. She was like a vision in the young men's eyes. The women they knew were plain, dressed themselves in worn-out clothing, and wandered through the wilderness.

Rahab was something to behold. "What she says is good," they thought, "and it is good to just look at her." It was like a dream. But, it was short lived. A loud knock on the door brought the two men back to reality.

There was no doubt in their minds that they had been discovered. "Hide us," they begged the woman.

"If you promise to save me and my household when your men take the city," Rahab bargained.

"We promise! Our life for yours."

Rahab quickly took the two men to the roof and hid them in stalks of flax. Then she opened the door for the king's soldiers who were now knocking with great impatience and loudly demanding that the door be opened.

"Bring forth the men who have come to you, for they have come to search out all the land," ordered the soldiers.

"True, men came to me, but I do not know where they came from; and when the gate was to be closed at dark, the men went out. Pursue them quickly, for you can still overtake them."

The searchers left in a hurry, and Rahab climbed to the roof. Strange are the ways of the Lord. To this harlot was revealed the truth which she witnessed to the Israelites.

"The Lord your God is he who is God in heaven above and on earth beneath," she said. "I know that the Lord had given you the land, and that the fear of you has fallen upon us. There is no courage left in any man because of you. Now swear to me by the Lord, that as I have dealt kindly with you, you also will deal kindly with my father's house."

"If you do not reveal this business of ours," promised the men, "then we will deal kindly with you when the Lord gives us the land."

Since her dwelling was near the top of the city wall, Rahab had to let the men out through the window and down to ground level by a scarlet rope.

"Go into the hills," she told them, "and hide yourselves there for three days until your pursuers have returned."

"Look," said one of the two, "when we come into the land bind this scarlet cord in your window and gather all your kin in your house. If anyone goes out the doors of your house into the street, his blood shall be upon his head. But everyone who is in your house will be saved."

And Rahab said the words which centuries later were echoed

from the lips of the purest virgin who was to bring Salvation to mankind, "According to your words, so be it."

Rahab sent the two fugitives away and, when the time came, she bound the scarlet cord in the window.

After spending three days in the hills the two men swam across the Jordan and reported to anxious Joshua:

"Truly, the Lord has given all the land into our hands; all the inhabitants of the land are faint-hearted because of us."

Joshua rejoiced. Early in the morning he set out with all the people. Spirits were high. They were marching again, and this time directly into the Promised Land which they thought God would give them now, without further delay.

They reached the Jordan River. The water of the river was high, turbulantly overflowing its banks. After marching for three days it was time for a pause. While people rested Joshua's officers went through the camp giving new commands.

"When you see the Ark of the Covenant of the Lord your God being carried by the Levitical priests, then you shall set out from your place and follow it. Do not go near it—keep a distance between you and the Ark, about two thousand cubits*."

"Sanctify yourselves," proclaimed Joshua. "Tomorrow the Lord will do wonders among you."

People were in an elated mood. At last their wanderings would be over, or so they thought.

Next morning the Ark of the Covenant was passed on before the people by the priestly procession. People followed the Ark at the commanded distance. Those who bore the Ark came to the Jordan. When the feet of the priests bearing the Ark dipped into the overflowing banks, the Red Sea miracle was repeated again. The waters coming down from above stood and rose up in a heap far off, and those flowing down toward the sea were wholly cut off. The priests stood on dry land in the midst of the Jordan until all the people passed over on dry ground.

When the last one passed Joshua called twelve men, one from

---

*Equivalent to approximately 3,000 feet or one kilometer.

each tribe, and made them carry twelve stones from the midst of the Jordan. He instructed the twelve to lay them in the place of the next lodging. Another twelve stones were piled up in the midst of the Jordan where the priests stood, as a memorial for following generations of where the water had been cut off.

Singing praises to the Lord, the Israelites reached Gilgal where they encamped. The Lord said to Joshua, "Today I have rolled away the reproach of Egypt from you." In Hebrew the name of the place Gilgal means "to roll."

Scripture says: "And on the morrow after the passover, they ate of the produce of the land, unleavened cakes and parched grain. And the manna ceased on the morrow, when they ate of the produce of the land; and the people of Israel had manna no more, but ate of the fruit of the land of Canaan that year."

The years of wandering were over, but the task of conquering the land was still ahead of them. The people did not realize that. Only Joshua knew it, but his faith and confidence in God's help did not waiver.

In the valley of Jericho Joshua lifted his eyes to the well-fortified city, with thick walls surrounding it. All the gates of Jericho were closed since they had crossed the Jordan. Suddenly he saw a man in front of him with a drawn sword in his hand.

"Are you one of us, or an adversary?" asked Joshua, approaching the stranger.

"No," said the the man. "But as a commander of the army of the Lord I have now come."

Joshua fell on his knees, bowing low with his face on the ground.

"Put off your shoes from your feet: for the place where you stand is holy."

Joshua took off his boots. Now he knew for sure, as the Lord had been with Moses, so he was with him.

The Voice of the Lord proposed a strange strategy for conquering the fortified city of Jericho, a strategy that seemed too foolish to be accepted by any army general. But Joshua did not question it. God had spoken, and he did exactly what God commanded. They had to go around the city in procession once a day for six days. Seven priests would bear the trumpets of rams' horns before the Ark. On the seventh day they had to go around the city seven times blowing the trumpets. It was the first psychological war the Lord had waged against the frightened and panicked people of Jericho.

When the Israelites were marching around Jericho for the seventh time on the seventh day and the trumpets gave a long blare, Joshua commanded the people to shout. And behold, the walls of Jericho crumbled and fell down. The city had been destroyed by the Israelites!

The inhabitants of Jericho were all killed, excepting Rahab and her father's household who were spared according to the promise. There were no casualties on the part of the Israelites. In the dizziness of their victory they were ready to attack the next city.

Besides getting drunk with pride over their first victory, some of them took booty and hid it. This was strictly forbidden. One man was found guilty. He and his whole household were mercilessly stoned by the crowd — another victim for the sins of all the rest. Israel felt at ease, the ransom had been paid.

It would be easy to capture another city, many suggested. Neighboring Ai was smaller in size and less populated. Why wait? Forge ahead and conquer it without losing any time! They attacked Ai. To their surprise they met fierce resistance. Sixty of the first lines were killed, and the Israelites fled away leaving their casualties behind.

Once again the Lord showed his people that only by relying on his help and not on their own strength would they advance.

Joshua, as well as the elders of Israel, tore their clothes in rage and fell on the ground. They spent the whole day in prayer and repentance.

"O Lord, what can I say when Israel has turned its back before the Canaanites! The Canaanites will surround us and wipe your name off the face of the earth. What will you do for your great name?"

This was not what the Lord had in mind. It was meant only as a lesson. "Arise," said the Voice of God. "Why have you fallen upon your face? Israel has sinned, they have violated the covenant. . . ."

The next day Joshua chose the men of valor to attack Ai again. He divided them into three groups: one would attack the city and pretend to be fleeing from the Canaanites just like the first time; the other two groups would lie in ambush. When Ai's defenders saw the Israelites fleeing, they chased after them, leaving the city without any men to protect it. At that time the men arose up from ambush and seized the city, burning it to the ground.

The Israelites, at least for the time being, learned a lesson and under Joshua's wise command, took one city after another. The conquered land was divided among the tribes.

Five lesser kings of Canaan threatened by the Israelites made an alliance among themselves to fight against Joshua. The battle was near Gibeon. The Lord threw stones from heaven upon the enemy, but the enemy would not give up. Joshua knew that when the sun went down the enemy would have time to regroup and that it would then be much harder to win the battle. So Joshua called to God in the sight of his army, "Sun, stand still over Gibeon, and, moon, you also over the valley of Aijalon."

So powerful was the voice of Joshua, his faith so deep, that it could not only move mountains, as was later told by Christ, but his faith was strong enough to halt the sun and moon on their course. The sun stood still, with its setting delayed at least a day, and the moon remained over the valley until the nation had conquered its adversaries.

Years passed. Joshua was an old man. It was time for him to rest. He summoned all Israel, their leaders, chief men, judges and officers, just as Moses did before his death. He addressed them, saying:

"Behold, I have alloted to you as an inheritance for your tribes those nations that remain to be conquered, along with the nations that I conquered for you. The Lord your God will drive them out before you, and you will possess their land. Be steadfast and keep the Law of Moses. If you disobey the Covenant of the Lord your God and serve other gods, the anger of the Lord will be kindled against you and you will perish quickly from off the good land which he has given you. Fear the Lord and serve him in sincerity and faithfulness."

When Joshua finished his lengthy advise and gave his blessing to the people, he sent them away — every man to his own inheritance. Joshua, son of Nun, the servant of the Lord, died at the age of one hundred-and-ten-years. They buried him in the hill country of Ephraim north of the mountain of Goath.

22. Gideon — the Man of Valor

Little by little the Israelites pushed the Canaanites toward "The Great Sea," the Mediterranean. They did not take all the land by battle and extinction of the original inhabitants. In some places they settled without much resistance and lived quite peacefully, at least for a while.

As the years proved, peaceful "coexistence" was often more harmful for the chosen people than wars and famine. Although the Lord warned them not to intermix with heathens, that rule was not always kept. Some Israelites took wives from the Canaan tribes and some Israel women married Canaanites. These mixed marriages weakened the Israelites' faith in the One True God. In households where marriages were mixed there often were two altars: one to the Lord God, God of Israel; anothed altar for pagan deities. Partly because the Israelites believed that the One True God was the God of Israelites only and not of gentiles, they did not try to convert heathens to their faith.

In a few generations the majority of Israelites abandoned belief in the One True God and began to worship a graven image, one they could see and touch, the pagan idol Baal. The cycle of forgetting the One True God, falling into wickedness, God's punishing them, and their repenting repeated itself again and again throughout Israel's history. To get his people on the right track, God sent another man of valor, Gideon. With great power and ferocity he destroyed the altar and image of Baal one day.

The Voice of God, silent for a long time, spoke again on this occasion to young Gideon. At that time the Israelites were oppressed by the Midianites. Listening to the Voice of God, Gideon gathered from the neighboring hills a thirty-two thousand man army.

On the day before battle the Voice of the Lord spoke again to Gideon. This time he ordered him to reduce his army to three hundred men and to disarm and dismiss the rest. Gideon did as the Lord commanded. The elders were not only upset, they thought Gideon had certainly lost his mind.

To choose three hundred braves from thirty-two thousand in such a short time would be an impossible task, unless it was done at random. But even now God showed Gideon the way: those men who drank from the river like dogs licking water with their tongues were set aside and dismissed; the others who drank from their cupped hands were the chosen ones.

To each of those hundred valiant men Gideon gave a brass trumpet and a jar with a torch set in it. At night when everyone was in deep sleep, Gideon ordered them to blow the trumpets as loud as possible, calling and shouting, "The sword of the Lord and of Gideon!" Three hundred men raced down the hill with lit torches in their hands, blasting noise in the air.

The shattering cries awakened the sleeping Midianites. In the darkness the lit torches looked like a flowing river of fire. When they saw this they thought that the enemy was coming in overwhelming numbers and strength. They fled toward the Jordan Valley as fast as their feet could carry them.

The conquest was made without a battle. The two enemy

rulers of the Midianites were killed. The Israelites were jubilant.

"Rule over us," they pleaded with Gideon, "you and your sons!"

"I will not rule over you, neither shall my sons," replied Gideon. "The Lord shall rule over you."

While Gideon was alive, people felt safe. They had a strong leader, a man on whose side was the Lord God himself.

Gideon was their judge for many years. When he died, leaving seventy sons, the question arose again, "Who shall rule Israel?" While sixty-nine brothers were holding a conclave to choose the new leader, the seventieth, named Abimelech, left them and went to his mother's kinsmen in Shechem, There he plotted against his brothers. Gathering menfolk, he attacked his brothers, killing them all except for the youngest, Jotham, who managed to escape.

Abimelech was a ruthless, bloodthirsty tyrant who waged many wars against his own people. During one battle he burned one thousand women and children locked in the crypt of a temple. Right after that he attacked another city and set it on fire. There he met his end from the hand of a woman who had climbed to the top of a building. When Abimelech passed by beneath, she threw a millstone on his head, crushing his skull.

Still conscious and seeing his end, Abimelech whispered an order to his armor-bearer, "Draw your sword and kill me, lest men say of me, 'A woman killed him.' "

Obeying the order, the young man thrusted his sword through his despotic ruler's heart. Abimelech was dead.

After him there was a succession of rulers who judged the Hebrews. The twelve tribes of Israel lived scattered in tent villages throughout the hills of Canaan. They did not unite into one power, and only during emergencies were they provided with a strong leader. In relatively peaceful days they had judges who decided on important matters, settling disputes among people.

By intermingling with other people, the Israelites did what was evil in the eyes of the Lord, and the Lord gave them into the hands of the Philistines for forty years.

What is today called "coexistence" was practiced in those days by the Hebrews, to their own destruction. The harder they tried to live peacefully with the Philistines, the more the heathens dominated the chosen people.

The Israelites were not united. Every man did what was right in his own eyes. For example, there was a certain man named Micah who had acquired great wealth. He built a shrine with an altar at which he was to worship the Lord. Upon this same altar he placed a carved image of Baal. Micah hired a priest, a Levite* who consented to perform elaborate ceremonies to both the One True God and Baal.

The Philistines, originally from Greek islands, occupied the territory near the Mediterranean Sea encompassing the cities of Gaza, Ashkelon, Ashdod, Ekron and Gezer. The Greeks named the land of the Philistines "Palestine."

They were people with their own culture and technical prowess. They knew how to cast iron, make war machines and iron chariots, skills unknown to Israelites. The Philistines were a vital and cunning nation pushing the Israelites, especially the tribe of Dan, northward out of the Promised Land.

23. Samson the Giant

During the time that Dan's tribe was oppressed by the Philistines, a son was born to a couple evicted from their homestead. His father, Manoah, called the boy Samson. His mother, who like Sara was childless for many years, dedicated her child to God, in accordance with an angel who appeared to the couple announcing:

"You shall conceive and bear a son. No razor shall come upon

---

*Levites belonged to the priestly order since the time of Moses and Aaron.

his head, for the boy shall be God's Nazarite* from birth. He shall begin to deliver Israel from the hands of the Philistines."

The happy couple asked the angel who looked just like an ordinary man, "What is your name, so that we may honor you when your words come true?"

"Why do you ask my name, seeing it is wonderful?" was the reply, and they did not see him anymore.

Realizing their great responsibility, Manoah and his wife raised their son with the greatest of care and piety, consecrating him to God. They taught him to love and to serve the Lord, the One True God.

Samson grew tall and strong. He was so superior in physical power that there was no match for him in the whole vicinity. He was a giant of a man with one weakness: he was made quite powerless by the charms of beautiful women. Much to his parents' dismay, Samson was spending too much time with the neighboring youths, the Philistines — more time with them than his religious upbringing dictated. Good-natured Samson enjoyed himself in their company, disregarding the mission foretold by the angel.

One day he told his parents that he had fallen in love with a Philistine girl from Timnah. The poor couple were stricken with grief. It was beyond their understanding how their religious son, who believed in the Lord and was consecrated to God, could choose a heathen woman for his bride.

"Aren't there beautiful girls among the Israelites?" they kept asking him. But Samson, with the heart and stubborness of youth, said to his parents, "None. Get her for me; for she pleases me well."

Worried about the kind of influence this heathen girl would have on their son who had been raised in such a religious atmosphere, Samson's parents set out on to the road to Timnah with Samson to make marriage negotiations with the girl's parents. Go-

---

*Nazarite in Hebrew means "consecrated." Samson was consecrated for life to the Nazarite vow which obliged him to abstain from drinking wine and from having his hair cut.

Finding the beast, he tore it apart like a kid.

ing through the vineyards of Timnah they heard a lion roaring. The Spirit of the Lord moved Samson, and he left his parents. Finding the beast, he tore it apart like a kid. Then he rejoined his parents as though nothing had happened, not even mentioning it.

The proposal of marriage was accepted. As a matter of fact, the bride's father even boasted about having the mightiest man for his son-in-law. Samson was well-pleased with his bride-to-be, and the wedding date was set.

When he and his parents were on the way back to Timnah for the wedding, Samson went out of his way to see the carcass of the lion. It was still there and in the lion's body was a swarm of bees and honey. Samson scraped out some honey and rejoining his parents, shared it with them.

There was a lavish wedding feast. According to Philistine tradition everyone was invited, the whole village. In the wedding party there were thirty young men none of whom Samson cared for a great deal. It was, however, a Philistine wedding, and the thirty men felt like an important part of the feast.

One usually successful way to degrade a groom was to get him intoxicated with wine so that he would make a fool of himself. But, to their dismay, Samson would not partake in wine, even though it was his own wedding. The thirty Philistines tried to provoke him in every possible way, but good-natured naive Samson did not take offense at anything.

Very frustrated, the men pestered Samson with riddles, but Samson remained calm. He had been in similar company a number of times and knew the answers before they could finish the puzzling problems. But enough was enough, even for the meekest! Samson stood up tall and mighty like an oak in the midst of saplings.

"Let me put a riddle to you," he said in a deep, fully controlled voice, the strength of which immediately quieted every drunken rascal.

"If you can tell me the answer within seven days of the feast, I will give you thirty linen garments; but if you cannot tell me what it is then you shall give me thirty festal garments."

Having thirty men, plus all the Philistines attending the wedding, to guess the riddle's answer within seven days time made the bargain seem like child's play.

"Ask your riddle that we may hear it," agreed the men gaily.

"Out of the eater came something to eat," slowly pronounced Samson, "but out of the strong came something sweet."

Everybody searched their minds quietly for a long time. Then they put their heads together to thrash out an answer. Three days passed, still no answer. On the fourth day the thirty men surrounded the beautiful bride with their threatening request:

"Entice your husband into telling us what the answer is, lest we burn you and your father's house with fire. Have you invited us here to rob us?"

Samson's wife wept in front of him, trying to cajole the answer from him. Each night during the seven days the feast lasted, she would weep when they were left alone, telling him that he hated her and did not hold any love for her by keeping such a secret in his heart. On the seventh day, not being able to withstand her pleas any longer, he told her the answer. She in turn told the answer of the riddle to her countrymen.

On the last day before sundown, the best man stood up and told the answer to a most attentive wedding party:

"What is sweeter than honey?

What is stronger than a lion?"

With reproof and anger Samson looked at his own young wife who had betrayed him at their wedding. He left the party and went straight to Ashkelon. There, at a similar wedding feast, he killed thirty men, stripped them of their festal garments and brought the robes to those who had answered his riddle. Taking his parents, he immediately left for his father's house leaving his wife behind.

In those days it was a disgrace for a woman to be deserted after the wedding, so her father hastily gave her to the best man in the wedding party.

But Samson could not forget his beautiful wife. He loved her and longed for her. At the time of the wheat harvest he took a kid as a peace offering and went to Timnah to bring his wife back with him. Entering his father-in-law's house, there was no welcome for Samson. His wife's father told him what happened — she was now the wife of a different man.

"From this day I shall be blameless in what I do against the Philistines," swore the enraged Samson.

His retaliation was strange. He caught three hundred foxes, turned them tail to tail and put a torch between each pair of tails. Then he set fire to the torches and let the foxes run into the standing wheat fields and into the olive orchards, burning everything to the ground. In reprisal, the angry Philistines punished Samson's wife and her father by burning them and their whole household alive.

Samson's first love affair ended. After slaughtering many Philistines, Samson went to Mount Etam and stayed there in a cave.

The Philistines could not forgive Samson. Likewise, Samson's mortal enemies were the Philistines. He brooded on top of the mountain, alone in seclusion.

Meanwhile Philistines were attacking the peaceful Judeans, all because of Samson's rage. They made one raid after another until the Judeans gave in. Three thousand armed Judeans gathered at the foot of Mount Etam. On the mountain top stood giant Samson.

"Have you forgotten that Philistines rule over us?" the Judeans called up to him.

Only after the men of Judah promised that they would not harm Samson, did he come down from the mountain and let himself be bound with new ropes and delivered to the Philistines as a criminal.

When the Philistines saw Samson captured and bound they shouted with joy, laughing and sneering at him with contempt. Samson could not stand it. His temper flared up. He felt a mysterious strength again fill every muscle of his body. To the surprise of the Philistines, he broke every rope and, using the jawbone of an ass picked up from the ground, he slew a thousand men. Philistines scattered like a swarm of bees.

Samson returned home. He became the judge for his people in Israel for twenty years.

The rulers of the Philistines could neither forgive nor forget their humiliation and decided to destroy Samson in one way or another. He was constantly watched and followed but, feeling physically superior, Samson did not care about it.

Then he fell into a trap. In the valley of Sorek there lived a beautiful Philistine, Delilah. When Samson saw her he fell in love with all the passion and power of a giant. He took her for his wife.

The Philistine elders called a special meeting. They recalled Samson's first wedding to the Philistine girl from Timnah. One of them knew to tell that this great and unconquerable giant was like beeswax in the hands of a woman.

Apparently Delilah did not love her giant husband the way he loved her. When the elders offered her money to deceive her husband, money meant more to her than his love or even his life. Her task was to find out the secret of Samson's unparalleled strength.

Day after day she begged Samson to disclose the secret. Her curiosity made Samson suspicious. He said it was no secret — he was just born to be strong, as she was born to be beautiful.

"Oh, but there are many secrets to being beautiful," she persisted. Every night she tried to persuade him in different ways to tell him from where his great strength came.

Tired of her constant nagging, he gave her all kinds of answers just to get peace. He told her that if she would bind him with seven bowstrings not yet dried, he would become as weak as any other man. Delilah did not hesitate to do this and then called the Philistines to come and get him. But Samson freed himself with no struggle at all. Delilah did not give up, persisting even more. Samson gave her similarly incorrect answers. She knew he was not telling her the truth. The whole thing became a game between them.

The elders of the Philistines, becoming impatient with her, threatened, "Either you get us the secret or we take your life."

Delilah used the most effective feminine weapon — tears. She cried, reproaching Samson very tenderly, "How can you say you love me when your mind is not with me? You have told me lies three times and still will not tell me where your great strength lies."

Samson was sad and his soul wearied. He loved Delilah so much that he wanted to be able to trust her and to be open with her. Although he never forgot the sad experience with his first wife, he reasoned that lovely Delilah was different.

"The razor has never come upon my head for I am a nazarite," he solemnly whispered to his most attentive and charming Delilah. "This means I am consecrated to God. If I am shaved, then my strength will leave me, and I shall become weak like any other man."

This was surely the truth! Delilah knew that she had not been fooled again. The next morning she went to the chiefs of the Philistines, reporting in all earnestness, "I have the secret now! Pay me the sum of money as we agreed, and Samson will be like a kid in your hands."

There was mutual distrust between her and the elders. "Come tonight and stay in hiding until I call you," she arranged. "Just be sure to bring your money with you when you come!"

Now it was a matter of life and death. Such was the agreement, if Samson should overcome the Philistines again, it would be her death.

In the evening Delilah adorned herself as lavishly as a goddess. She was so sweet and loving toward Samson that he considered himself the luckiest man on earth to possess such a precious wife. Full of gentleness, she lulled him to sleep, his head cradled in her lap. But when Samson, filled with love and happiness, was peacefully asleep, she gave a signal to a man. The culprit was a professional barber with razor in hand who quickly shaved off the seven locks on Samson's head and then, just as quickly disappeared.

"Samson, the Philistines are upon you," she called, shaking him by the shoulders and pushing him with all her might from herself. Samson awoke. Delilah called again in a harsh, cold tone, "Philistines! Philistines!"

Samson could not believe the change in his wife's voice from the tender lulls he had seemingly just heard. The song of a dove turned into the screeching of a jackal. So cold and cunning it sounded, so harsh, that Samson thought it must be because she was frightened.

"I will break loose as at other times and shake myself free," self-assured, he tried to console his beautiful and beloved wife.

A never before experienced coolness was breezing over Samson's head. He felt strangely naked. With the familiar gesture, he tried to brush the locks away from his face. Instead he touched his bare head. It was naked! Indeed, his locks, all his hair, was gone. Giving a quick glance at Delilah, standing pale and frightened with guilt upon her face and clutching money in her fists, Samson understood. . . .

But before he could ask the stone-cold Delilah why she had done it, the Philistines seized him. This time he could not shake them off, his strength had left him. The Philistines tied him and, with a searing hot metal bar held close to his face, they put his eyes out. Samson was irreparably blind.

Gloating about the victory over their long time enemy, the Philistines still did not take any chances. They bound Samson with bronze fetters and took him to Gaza. There he was a slave in a prison, blind and helpless, turning the huge stone of the grinding mill.

Several months passed. The hair on Samson's shaved head was growing back. Before too long his locks reached shoulder length.

One day the Philistines were celebrating a great feast. It

started in the temple with sacrifices to Dagon, their god. A multitude of people took part in their pagan festivity with drinking and dancing in an orgy of wild pleasure. When the chiefs were tired and bored with the merrymaking, one of them suggested, "Summon Samson that he may make sport for us."

That sounded like a promise of great amusement. After all, hadn't their god delivered Samson into their hands?

"Our god has given into our hands Samson, our enemy," said one of the elders, "the ravager of our country who has slain many of us."

They brought Samson from the prison, they mocked and slapped him. Their pleasure was a rare one and was the highlight of the feast. Under the influence of wine and the delirium of triumph, they called insults at Samson in the presence of three thousand men and women, as well as all the rulers of the Philistines. They mocked not only Samson, but also his God, the Lord.

"O Lord God," whispered Samson, "remember me, I pray thee. Strengthen me, I pray thee, only this once that I may be avenged upon the Philistines for my two eyes."

He said to the boy who was leading him, since Samson could not see, "Let me feel the pillars on which the building rests, that I may lean against them."

The lad brought him between two huge pillars, the main supports of the big dome.

"Let me die with the Philistines," Samson whispered a prayer quietly but with great intensity and all the fervor of his soul.

The Philistines in the noise of laughter and cheering could not hear his words, but they saw his lips moving.

"Look, he is praying to his Lord," someone sneered.

Samson felt strength return to his body and stream into every blood vessel. Putting his large hands on each pillar, he crouched low and pushed with all his might. The pillars gave in. Cracking and crumbling, they collapsed and with them the whole building. Underneath the ruins and rubble lay all the rulers of the Philistines, along with thousands of people, including Samson. All were crushed to death. Scripture says: "The dead whom he slew at his death were more than those whom he had slain during his life."

Samson's brothers dug him out of the ruins of the pagan temple and buried his body in the tomb of his father, Monoah.

24. Naomi and Ruth

In the days of the judges there was a famine in the land of Canaan. One year crops were destroyed by drought and the next year by swarms of locusts. A certain man, Elimelech from Bethlehem, and his wife Naomi decided to try their luck in some other place where the pastures were still green. They took their two little sons and went to Moab. Although Moabites were not on friendly terms with Israelites, the humble peasant family was well-received and even allowed to acquire some land.

Many years passed, the Scripture says ten, and the sons of Elimelech and Naomi married Moabite girls, Orpha and Ruth.

Elimelech died in the land of Moab and soon after him both his sons died. Naomi was left with two daughters-in-law. Full of sorrow, she decided to go back to the land of her birth, Bethlehem in Judea. Her daughters-in-law were still very young and attractive women and since Naomi did not have any sons to marry them, she urged the girls to leave her and return to their parents.

"Go, return, each of you to your mother's house," said the bereaved Naomi. "May the Lord deal kindly with you, as you have dealt with the dead and me. The Lord grant that you may find a home, each of you in the house of your husband!"

But the girls, weeping, said to Naomi, "No, we will return with you to your people."

Naomi pleaded with her daughters-in-law, "No, my daughters, for I would grieve deeply for you, for the hand of the Lord has gone against me."

Orpha kissed her mother-in-law goodbye and returned to her father's house. But Ruth clung to Naomi and would not leave her. Still weeping, she begged Naomi, "Do not force me to leave you; for where you go I will go, and where you lodge I will lodge; your people shall be my people, and your God my God."

Naomi saw that Ruth was steadfast and because of this she did not urge her to return to her kin.

When they reached Bethlehem some of Naomi's old neighbors saw her and recognized her although she had grown old. They asked among themselves, "Is this Naomi?"

"Do not call me Naomi. Call me Mara (Bitter), for the Almighty has dealt very bitterly with me."

It was the season of harvesting when the two women returned to Bethlehem. Ruth asked Naomi, "Let me go and glean among the ears of grain."

"Go, my daughter," answered Naomi.

Ruth gleaned in the field belonging to a kinsman of Elimelech named Boaz, a very wealthy man.

Boaz went around noon each day to see the reapers. He was not a young man any more, probably middle aged. He spotted Ruth right away and although she was dressed very poorly, nearly in rags, her beauty did not escape his keen eye.

"Whose maid is this?" he asked the overseer.

"She asked me to gather the sheaves after the reapers," explained the overseer. She is Ruth, a Moabitess, who came with Naomi. She has worked from early morning until now without resting a moment."

Boaz approached Ruth and said, "Listen, my daughter, do not go to glean in another field or leave this one, but keep close to my maidservants. I have charged my young men not to molest you. When you are thirsty go to the vessels and drink."

Ruth, full of gratitude, fell on her face and said to him, "Why have I found favor in your eyes, that you should take notice of me, when I am a foreigner?"

Boaz told her all she had done for her mother-in-law since

the death of her own husband. He knew that she left her father and mother and her native land and went to people she did not know.

"May the Lord recompense you for what you have done and a full reward be given to you by the Lord, the God of Israel, under whose wings you have come to take refuge," Boaz told her.

At mealtime Boaz told her to join his servantmaids to eat some bread and to dip her morsel in the wine.

After the meal Ruth gleaned again until evening when she beat out what she had gleaned, amounting to a little over one bushel of barley. This amount she was allowed to take home with her. Grateful for the kindness shown her, she returned to her mother-in-law.

Naomi was surprised and asked, "Where did you glean today? Blessed is the man who noticed you."

Ruth returned day after day to the same field and continued to gather the grain after the reapers until the end of the barley harvest when all the grain was laid into the barns. Boaz was continually aware of her and exceedingly pleased by her presence.

One day Boaz said to Ruth, "My daughter, all the people who dwell within the gates of my city know that you are a virtuous woman."

When the city elders heard of the proposed marriage between Boaz and Ruth they said, "May the Lord make this woman who is coming into your house an example of virtue in Ephrata and may she have a famous name in Bethlehem."

Boaz married Ruth in a great wedding feast, after which the prophecy came true. Her name and virtue is proclaimed in churches until this day.

Marrying Ruth brought Boaz, an Israelite from the tribe of Judah, into union with a woman of the gentiles. They had a son and named him Obed. He was the father of Jesse who in turn was father of David, the king. Centuries later Christ was born from the root of Jesse, the house of David.

25. "Samuel! Samuel!"

In front of the temple in Shiloh was a woman kneeling in prayer. Her nearly-black hair flowed down her shoulders, over her waist and hips, touching the ground. She was wringing her hands as her lips moved silently. Her large brown eyes burned as those of a madwoman.

The old bleary-eyed priest, Eli, obscurely sitting behind the doorpost of the temple, observed the woman for a long time before losing his patience.

"How long will you be drunken? Put away your wine!" he said scornfully to the woman in distress.

"No, my lord," she wailed, "I am a woman sorely troubled. I have drunk neither wine nor strong drinks, but have been pouring out my soul before the Lord. I am crying out of great anxiety and vexation."

She told the old priest that she was Hannah, the wife of Elkanah. Every year they came from Ramah to Shiloh to offer sacrifices: her husband, his second wife with her numerous children, and she the barren one. Every time they made this long journey the other wife bragged about her fertility, scorning Hannah for her barrenness. She did it out of jealousy because Elkanah loved Hannah much more than the woman who gave him many offspring. Her husband kept asking Hannah why she was grieving. Didn't he mean more to her than ten sons? But she was in distress because the Lord would not open her womb.

Eli listened to the poor woman's outpouring of her soul and took pity on her. When Hannah finished her lament, Eli joined her in pleading with the Lord. They prayed together.

"O Lord of Hosts!" called Hannah vehemently, "If thou wilt indeed look on the affliction of thy maidservant and remember me by giving me a son, then I will give him to you all the days of his life."

Blessing her, the old near-sighted priest said, "Go in peace.

May the God of Israel grant the petition which you have made to him."

This was enough for Hannah. In deep faith and with renewed spirit she left Eli and joined the party which was just ready to take their picnic meal. She sat on the grass next to the spread out tablecloth and ate with the family.

Elkanah looked at his beloved wife and was pleasantly surprised. For several days Hannah, in her sorrow, had not touched food. Now her depression was gone, her eyes sparkled. After she ate, a beautiful blush returned to her cheeks.

There was a new peace in Hannah and the joy that was lost for such a long time returned. They went home to Ramah. In due time Hannah gave birth to a son. She called him Samuel which means "heard of God" or "asked of God."

"I have asked him from the Lord," she said.

When the child was weaned and three years old, Elkanah and Hannah took him, along with a young ox, three bushels of flour and a skin of wine, to Shiloh.

"Oh my lord!" said the happy mother to the old priest, Eli. "As you live, my lord, I am the woman who was standing here in your presence praying to the Lord. For this I prayed, and the Lord granted my petition. Therefore I have lent him to the Lord for as long as he lives."

Eli, Hannah and Elkanah worshipped the Lord together, giving praise and thanksgiving to him for the man-child. During this time the spirit came upon Hannah. She prophesied in a prototype of the Magnificat, chanting with a grateful heart:

"My heart exults in the Lord;
my strength is exalted in the Lord,
my mouth derides my enemies,
because I rejoice in thy salvation.

"There is none holy like the Lord,
there is none besides thee;
there is no rock like our God. . .

"The adversaries of the Lord
shall be broken to pieces;
against them he will thunder in heaven.

"The Lord will judge the ends of the earth;
he will give strength to his king,
and exalt the power of his anointed."

The old priest Eli and Elkanah stared at Hannah while she chanted the prophecy in exaltation, holding her man-child in her arms. When she finished she kissed her son and handed him to the holy man. Both parents returned to Ramah, and the boy remained to minister to the Lord under the guidance of Eli.

In the coming years Hannah was blessed again and again with more sons and daughters. But Samuel did not know them for he grew up in the temple.

In the same temple serving the Lord were two unworthy priests, both Eli's sons, Hophni and Phinehas. Their sin was great before the eyes of the Lord for they treated the offering of the people with contempt. Eli knew about it, but being old and soft-hearted, he was overly indulgent with his sons. He rebuked them mildly, but the sons paid no attention to their father's reprimands. They had fear neither of their father nor of the Lord God.

One night Samuel, then fifteen, was sleeping on his mat near the temple door when he heard a voice call his name, "Samuel."

Thinking it must be the old priest who called him, Samuel scampered to his feet and, in the dim light of the sacrificial lamp in front of the Ark, he hurried to Eli's chamber. There he found the old priest asleep. Samuel woke him up.

"Here I am, for you called me," he said to Eli.

"I did not call you, my son. Go lie down again," answered Eli, thinking that Samuel had been dreaming.

Samuel returned to his mat and lay down. It was strange for he knew someone had called him as the voice was so penetrating and unforgettable.

As soon as he started to doze off the same voice called again, "Samuel! Samuel!"

This time he was sure he heard it. He quickly ran to Eli and, shaking the old man who was already snoring, he repeated, "Here I am, for you called me."

"I did not call you, my son, return and sleep," Eli replied. He thought the boy had exhausted himself and must be having nightmares. But when the same thing happened a third time, Eli dismissed his previous thoughts and perceived that the Lord, who had been silent for a very long time, must be calling the boy.

"Go lie down," he repeated to Samuel. "If he calls you, say, 'Speak, Lord, for thy servant hears.' "

Again when Samuel was on his mat lying in the darkness of the night, he heard the same voice, the Voice which Adam heard in Paradise, the Voice which spoke to Abraham and Moses.

"Samuel! Samuel!" called the majestic Voice.

"Speak, for thy servant hears!" answered Samuel, all trembling.

"Behold," the voice was pentrating Samuel's soul and mind, "I am about to do such a thing in Israel as will make the two ears of all who hear it ring. Tell Eli that I am about to punish his house forever because of the iniquity about which he knew. His sons were blaspheming God and he did not restrain them. Therefore I swear that the iniquity of Eli's house shall never be expiated by sacrifice or offering."

His eyes wide open, Samuel lay until morning, not being able to make the slightest move. At daybreak he had to gather all his strength to get up and open the doors of the house of the Lord. There Eli came to the boy and asked him what he had heard. But Samuel was afraid to relay the message. Eli insisted, and Samuel finally told him everything.

"It is the Lord," Eli said, accepting the message in humble submission. "Let him do what seems good to him."

Nothing happened immediately. Quite to the contrary, everything went on just like before. Perhaps God intended to give this time to the house of Eli as a chance to repent and return to God.

Meanwhile Samuel grew up to be a young man. From Dan to Beersheba it was known that he was a chosen prophet of the Lord. And the Lord revealed himself to Samuel.

More years passed and the oppressions of the Philistines increased to the point that Israel went out to battle their enemies. In this battle the Israelites were defeated, losing about four thousand men.

When the tribes returned to their camp the elders of Israel said, "Let us bring the Ark of the Covenant of the Lord here from Shiloh, that he may come among us and save us from the power of our enemies."

They brought the Ark from Shiloh to the battlefield. When the troops saw it they let out a great shout, and the mountains rang with their loud voices. Eli's two sons, the unworthy priests, were in procession with the other priests carrying the Ark of the Covenant of God.

When the Philistines heard the noisy shouting and found out that the Ark of God was in the front lines with the battling Israelites, they became afraid. The leaders said to their troops, "Take courage, be men and fight!"

In renewed attack the Philistines defeated the Israelites again. Thirty thousand were slain and the rest put to flight. The Ark was captured.

Out of breath from running, a messenger came to Eli who was sitting by the roadside in Shiloh awaiting news from the battlefield. Eli was a very old man now, ninety-eight. He was worn out physically because of wars, but most of all, spiritually because of the corruption of his own sons and his people.

"Your two sons, Hophni and Phineas, are dead," reported the courier, his clothes torn and dust upon his head. "The Ark of God has been captured as well."

Hearing this shocking news caused Eli to fall backward from his seat, breaking his collarbone. He died instantly.

Eli had judged Israel forty years. His successor was Samuel. The nation was defeated, troops were scattered, and the spirit of the people was very low. They needed a new strong leader, but Samuel was not a man of war. He was an ordained priest, a contemplative, a man of prayer. Ironically, the demand of the times was for a strong militarist. There was nothing even near that in the quiet manner of Samuel, the man to whom the Lord revealed himself.

The still-alive or wounded soldiers returned to their homes and plowing-fields which had been left in the care of the women and children. The spirit of the Israelites was at its lowest ebb. The Ark of the Covenant — symbol of freedom, holiness and all that was sacred, — their direct tie with with the Lord — this was in the hands of their idolatrous enemy. The tribes of Jacob were disorganized, scattered, defeated. Everybody looked to Samuel for an answer. The only answer he knew was reliance on God's power and prayer.

"Gather all Israel to Mizpah," Samuel told the sons of Israel. "And I will pray to the Lord for you."

People gathered in Mizpah for prayer and penitence. They purified themselves with water, fasted, prayed and repented, saying, "We have sinned against the Lord."

Hearing that the Israelites had gathered in Mizpah, the Philistines came to attack them.

"Do not cease to cry to the Lord," pleaded the sons of Israel with their prophet. Samuel prayed and sacrified a young lamb as a burnt offering to the Lord.

While the offering was still burning, with Samuel wrapped in prayer and the Israelites lamenting around him, the Philistines drew near them for an attack, "but the Lord thundered with a mighty voice that day against the Philistines and threw them into confusion."

The Ark of the Covenant was still in the hands of the Philistines. When the enemy captured it in battle, they placed it in the temple of Dagon, as an offering to Dagon, their god to whom they believed they owed their victory.

Next morning, when they went into their temple, they found

the idol lying prostrate on the ground before the Ark. The Lord afflicted them with many evils on account of the Ark. Many Philistines died and from the fields came mice in great multitude, causing fear and confusion among the people.

After the Ark had been with the Philistines for seven months and they were troubled with one pestilence after another, they resolved to return the Ark of God to the Israelites. They laid it upon a cart and, taking two young cows, yoked them to the cart.

The cows made straight for Beth-shemesh, and the Ark was brought again into the hands of the Israelites. Great was their joy when the Levites took charge of the Ark again!

"If you will return to the Lord with all your heart and serve him only, he will deliver you from the hands of the Philistines," Samuel told them.

The Israelites humbled themselves before God, and the Lord took pity upon them and gave them such victory over the Philistines in the next battle that for many years there was peace and fertility in the land.

Chapter V

The Time of Kings

(circa 1095-588 B.C.)

26. Saul

Every year Samuel trod roads on a circuit to Bethel, Gilgal and Mizpah, ministering to his people and deciding on grave matters. He always returned to his hometown, Ramah, where the Ark of the Covenant was now, since Shiloh remained in the hands of the Philistines.

He was getting old and he made his sons judges. But, like the sons of Eli, they did not follow the way of their father. Rather, they took bribes from people and perverted justice. The elders of Israel were rightly concerned; the people were multiplying and disorganized tribes scattered over the numerous hills of Canaan. They were not united and were vulnerable to attack from inside or out. The elders brought the matter to Samuel's attention.

"Behold, you are old and your sons do not walk in your way," they said. "Appoint for us a king to govern us like all the nations."

Such talk displeased Samuel and he told the people that their only king was the Lord, only on his help and power should they rely. But the elders insisted, saying, "Give us a king!"

Distressed, Samuel turned to the Lord in prayer and supplication.

"Harken to their voices," answered the Lord, "Only solemnly warn them about the ways of a king."

Samuel, calling the elders together for a meeting, told them that a king would be their punishment. He further warned them that a king would rule over them with an iron hand, burden them with heavy taxes and would cause them to cry and lament.

But the elders still demanded, "Give us a king!"

Samuel dismissed the elders, sending each to his own town. In Gibeah there was a wealthy Benjamite Kish who had a very handsome son named Saul. The Scripture says: "There was not a man among the people of Israel more handsome than he; from shoulders upward he was taller than any of the people."

The young man was as spoiled as he was handsome, though. On good days he was most pleasant, the happiest and friendliest man ever known. But when things did not quite go his way he would withdraw to his tent. Sitting close to the entrance he would sulk, sometimes for a whole day or even longer. When he came out of hiding, he was once again as brilliant as sunshine. His friends tolerated his whims — after all it was the privilege of the rich and handsome to be difficult at times. But what were just caprices in boyhood and the whims of youth became much deeper disturbances in later years.

Samuel was on the lookout for a king. When he met Saul, who was searching for his father's lost asses with his servant, Samuel felt a definite stirring in his heart and instantly knew he had found a king for the Israelites. This attractive man, tall and handsome to behold, must be their king. He anointed Saul and presented him to the assembly. The people were pleased.

"God bless our king!" they shouted with joy.

When Saul left Samuel, the newly anointed king was a different man: "God gave him another heart." God's blessing was upon Saul. He not only succeeded in battle against the Philistines, he also became a prophet— a special gift of the Holy Spirit which God bestowed upon him.

People liked Saul. They trusted him and rejoiced in his victories over the Moabs, Ammonites, Edomites and Philistines. He was a valiant king and delivered the Israelites from their enemies.

Saul's oldest son, Jonathan, was his father's constant companion on the battlefield. He was given by his kingly father one thousand armored men whom Jonathan trained with great zeal. Jonathan was very much like his father: handsome and eager, but dizzy with new power. Being bored just drilling his one thousand men, he — without his father's knowledge — went into attack on the well-prepared Philistine troops in Geba. Saul had to come and rescue his son from defeat.

Saul was preparing a large attack on the Philistines, but so were the Philistines against Saul's troops. Everyone was ready for battle except Samuel. The old high priest was somewhere tarrying. No one could find the old prophet and they did not dare to venture into battle without his blessing of the troops, nor without prayers and sacrifice on the altar.

Saul waited seven days at Gilgal and his patience was running out. He saw from the top of the hill how the Philistines were getting better prepared with each day. With every hour their weapons, swords and javelins glittered brighter in the sun. But Samuel was somewhere hiding in one of the numerous caves — no one could find him.

To wait any longer would be to endanger the whole army, thought Saul. Exasperated and despairing, Saul went to the altar himself to make a burnt offering, which only an ordained priest could perform.

As soon at the offering was finished, Samuel, enraged about the sacrilege, stood in front of Saul.

"You have done foolishly," said Samuel to his king. "Now your kingdom shall not continue. The Lord has sought out a man after his own heart and has appointed him to be prince over his people, because you have not done what the Lord has commanded of you."

Samuel went from Gilgal to Gibeah of Benjamin. Saul was troubled. He did not have enough courage to attack the Philistines now. His spirit was low, and he needed time for healing. The new kingship was endangered. Saul took his son Jonathan, along with his best six hundred armed men and followed Samuel to Gibeah.

There Saul pitched tents for himself and his men and lived just like the rest, in humble simplicity. Although a king, Saul never lived in a palace. All his life he was more a general of his army than a king. All the days of his ruling he had to fight one battle after another. This made his life full of hardship and kept him on the alert all the time.

It was very rarely now that Saul would see the old blear-eyed Samuel. Still, one day Samuel found his way to Saul's tent.

"The Lord has sent me to anoint you king over his people Israel," proclaimed the old man.

Saul rejoiced. This meant he was still anointed king and that God himself was on this side. Samuel came with an important message from the Lord: attack the tribes of Amalek who so many times had molested the Israelites, especially when they were coming out of Egypt.

"Do not spare any of them," warned Samuel, "but kill both man and woman, infant and suckling, ox, sheep, camel and ass."

Full of new courage Saul summoned and defeated the Amelites. The war gain was tremendous and Saul could not resist temptation. He slew captured people, but spared their king Agag, taking him prisoner. Besides that, he kept the best sheep and oxen and all that was good for himself.

Before long Samuel received the message from the Voice: "I repent that I have made Saul king. He has turned back from following me."

Samuel was angry. Will that man never learn? Doesn't he see his own destruction? All night long Samuel cried to the Lord. Early in the morning he set out on the road to find Saul.

On the Mount of Carmel Saul celebrated his victory. There he told his subjects to build a monument to himself. When the feast of victory was over Saul left Carmel and went to Gilgal.

There Samuel, the messenger of God, and the king met. Seeing his prophet, Saul rushed to him calling, "Blessed be you to the Lord! I have performed the commandment of the Lord."

"What is this bleating of sheep in my ears and lowing of oxen which I hear?" asked Samuel angrily.

Saul tried to defend himself saying that he had utterly destroyed all Amaleks and took their king Agag prisoner. But people took the best of the spoils — sheep and oxen — to sacrifice to the Lord in Gilgal. After all, he wanted only to please his people.

"Behold, obeying is better than sacrifice," answered Samuel. "And to harken, than the fat of rams. For rebellion is as the sin of divination and stubborness is as iniquity and idolatry."

"Because you have rejected the word of the Lord, he has also rejected you as king."

Saul was distressed. He realized that he had sinned and transgressed the commandment. He asked Samuel, "I pray, pardon my sin and return with me that I may worship the Lord."

But his plea was in vain.

Samuel ordered to bring out King Agag. Upon seeing him, strength returned to Samuel's body. He did what he had never done before in his whole long life — he grasped a sword and slashed King Agag to pieces.

Samuel returned to Ramah, and Saul, in the gloomiest of moods, to his own house in Gibeah.

27. The Anointing of the Shepherd

Samuel loved Saul very deeply and grieved over him. Days, weeks, months passed. Samuel did not come out of the temple nor touch his food. From the many tears he shed for Saul his eyes became even dimmer. His hollow cheeks became grooved from the constant stream of tears.

"How long will you grieve over Saul," asked the Voice of the Lord, "seeing I have rejected him as king? Fill your horn with oil and go. I will send you to Jesse the Bethlehemite. I have provided for myself a king from among his sons."

To anoint another king while the one reigning is still well and alive would be treason, and Samuel was fully aware of this.

"How can I?" he asked the Lord. "If Saul hears of it he will kill me!"

"Take a heifer with you," was God's simple reply, "and say, 'I have come to sacrifice.' "

Samuel got up and, taking a heifer, was on his way to Bethlehem. From Ramah to Bethlehem was at least twenty miles* if journeying in a straight line, but over the hills on winding paths through the valleys the distance was much further. It took Samuel several days to reach Bethlehem.

Entering Jesse's home, he bowed in the customary greeting of SHALOM, "peace be with you." It was an honor for a house to receive the prophet of Israel, especially the old priest Samuel whose fame has spread over the whole country.

Samuel prepared the sacrifice and asked Jesse and his sons to take part in it. After the offering Samuel asked the host to present his sons to him. Jesse was puzzled but did not dare to contradict nor even question the elderly prophet.

Jesse started the review of his sons. The first-born son was Eliab. Even Samuel's dimmed eyes could recognize that Eliab was an attractive man, stalwart, handsome, and self-assured with an air of confidence about him.

"Do not look as his appearance nor the height of his stature," was the Lord's advice in the depth of Samuel's heart. "I have rejected him for the Lord sees not as a man sees. Man looks at outward appearances but the Lord looks into the heart."

Seven of Jesse's sons marched by Samuel. None of them were acceptable to the Lord.

"Are all your sons present?" the old man asked of his host.

"There remains the youngest, but he is tending the sheep."

"Fetch him for we will not sit down until he comes here."

"Impossible!" Jesse thought to himself, and so thought his seven sons. This youngest was an odd fellow. Constantly playing his reed, whistling or singing songs never heard before, he was considered a dreamer and one not to be taken seriously.

The father and brothers had forgotten the story of Joseph, also a deamer. Or, if they had not forgotten it, for it was told very

---

*32.18 kilometers.

often at family gatherings, they saw no correlation between the two.

"Bring him," repeated Samuel to the puzzled father.

The servants went to fetch the shepherd boy from the fields of Bethlehem. When the bushy-haired youth, with sun-tanned ruddy cheeks and two large bright eyes full of wonder and zeal, stood before Samuel, the Voice of the Lord spoke in the prophet's heart, "Arise and anoint him!"

Samuel did not hesitate. In the presence of Jesse and all his sons, Samuel anointed the youngest offspring.

"What is your name?" affectionately asked the old man, his shaky hand still resting on the kneeling lad's head.

"David."

The Spirit of the Lord came upon David and remained with him. Samuel gave careful instruction to the newly anointed David, warning Jesse and his sons as well about the secrecy of what happened. But the warning was not necessary. All of them, especially David, knew the importance of silence. His mission completed, Samuel returned to Ramah, and David to his father's flock.

On the hillsides of Bethlehem David poured out his heart into new and more beautiful songs. He carved himself an instrument out of a piece of wood, fastening some strings to it. The finished product resembled a lyre.

Having full confidence in the Lord, and the faith and trust that only a pure innocent heart could possess, he sang these words which flowed spontaneously from his heart:

The Lord is my shepherd, I shall not want;
He makes me lie down in green pastures.
He leads me beside still waters; he restores my soul.
He leads me in paths of righteousness for his
*   name's sake. . . .*
Surely goodness and mercy shall follow me all the
*   day's of my life;*
and I shall dwell in the house of the Lord forever.
(Ps. 23)

Spending days in the blazing sun and shivering in the cool breeze of evening in the open fields, David observed nature, the expanse of the sky and the greatness of the firmament. He was thinking about creation from the first day to the last on which God created man according to his likeness. David's heart burst out into new song:

> O Lord, our Lord, how majestic is thy name on all
>   the earth!
> Thou whose glory above the heavens is chanted by
>   the mouth of babes and infants. . . .
> When I look at thy heavens, the work of thy
>   fingers, the moon and the stars which thou
>   has established;
> What is man that thou art mindful of him and the
>   son of man that thou dost care for him?
> Yet thou has made him little less than God,
>   and dost crown him with glory and honor.
> Thou has given him dominion over the works of
>   thy hands;
> Thou has put all things under his feet, all sheep and
>   oxen, and also beasts of the field, the birds
>   of the air, and the fish of the sea, whatever
>   passes along the paths of the sea.
> O Lord, our Lord, how majestic is thy name
>   on all the earth! (Ps. 8)

David spent his lonely days and nights in the fields of Bethlehem guarding his secret. He dared only whisper it to his sheep, waiting and wondering when the Lord would call him.

Saul was falling into another spell of melancholy. Everything came to a standstill when the king brooded in his chamber. The king's servants were concerned about getting him out of the blackness of his mood. Everything possible was tried to draw him out of depression.

When it seemed as though they had run out of remedies, one

of the king's servants suggested bringing a singer and a lyre musician to entertain the king. It was hoped that the sound of beautiful music would work as therapy on the king's troubled spirit since everything else had failed.

"Find a man who can play well," said the sad king, "and bring him to me."

The same servant, full of hope, recommended with high praise Jesse and the Bethlehemite's son, David, who could play the lyre and sing beautiful songs. Besides being a skillful musician, he was "a man of valour, a man of war, prudent in speech, a man of good presence, and the Lord is with him."

Saul sent his man to fetch David and bring him to court. When David saw the king's messengers coming to his father's field to take him to Saul, his mind rambled with questions: "What will happen to me? Is God calling me already? Is my time at hand? What kind of turn will life take for me?"

When Saul saw David he liked the bright-eyed, ruddy-cheeked shepherd boy. David's singing, accompanied by the music of his own lyre, was very soothing to Saul's restless mind and brought calmness to his distressed spirits. Saul liked the goodlooking boy. When he liked someone, he tended to be most generous toward them.

He made David his personal armor-bearer, a greatly esteemed and very high position.

"Let David remain in my service, for he has found favor in my sight," was the message Saul sent to Jesse, David's father.

Many courtiers frowned upon the selection of David as the king's armor-bearer, but there was nothing they could do about it. Saul wanted David near him. Whenever the king showed signs of melancholy, David played his lyre. The evil spirits tormenting the king departed, and he was well and happy again.

28. Goliath — A Fearsome Giant

There were not many peaceful days during Saul's reign. The Philistines, old enemies of the Israelites, attacked them with renewed force. They gathered their army together on one side of the mountain with the valley lying just below. On the other side of the valley, atop another mountain, Saul's army mustered its troops.

Among the Philistines there was a fearsome giant named Goliath who came every morning to the valley, daring the Israelites to send out a man to match him in combat. Scripture says that the ten foot Goliath

> "had a helmet of bronze on his head, and he was
> armed with a coat of mail, and the weight of the
> coat was five thousand shekels of bronze. And he
> had greaves of bronze upon his legs, and a javelin
> of bronze slung between his shoulders. And the
> shaft of his spear was like a weaver's beam, and
> his spear's head weighed six hundred shekels of
> iron."

This giant, clad in armor from head to toe, came out twice daily from the Philistine camp, morning and evening, and challenged anyone to meet him in single combat.

"Give me a man!" shouted Goliath. "Let him fight me hand to hand. If he is able to kill me, we will be your servants. But, if I prevail and kill him, you will serve us."

The Israelites trembled with fear. For forty days Goliath defied them. There was no one in all Israel who would accept the challenge. Saul himself went to the battlefied, but even he did not dare stand against this frightening giant.

While Saul was on the battlefied David went home to see his father and to tend his sheep. Three of David's older brothers were in Saul's army, and the aging Jesse worried about them. He sent David to the battlefield with provisions — some loaves of bread, meat and wine for his sons — with the plea for David to return soon and to bring news of the war.

As David spoke with his brothers, the formidable giant Goliath came out and took his stand as on other mornings, roaring his challenge like an angry lion. David listened. Hearing the insults, blood rushed to his head. The veins on David's temple swelled and his heart beat faster and faster.

"Surely he has come to defy Israel," said the men around David. "The king will shower with great riches the man who kills him. Saul will even bestow his daughter upon such a brave warrior."

"Who is this uncircumsized Philistine that he should defy the armies of the living God?" demanded the young, enraged David.

When David's older brother Eliab heard the question he grew angry. The last thing he and his brothers wanted was to be embarrassed in front of their fellow soldiers by their ranting brother.

"Why have you come here?" asked Eliab his youngest brother with reproach. "And with whom have you left those few sheep in the wilderness? I know your pride and the evil in your heart. You have come down to see the battle!"

Although David was just about the right age to become a soldier, his duty, as the youngest son, was to tend the family's flock. That was what Eliab was reminding him. However, David's words were quickly repeated to the king. Saul, a great warrior, knew how hopeless the situation was. He sent for David.

Standing in front of the king, David bravely said, "Let no man's heart fail because of him."

He told Saul that he would go and fight this bragging giant.

"But you are just a lad, and he has been a man of war since his youth," wondered Saul.

David's courage did not falter. He told Saul how he had killed a lion and a bear when they attacked his father's sheep. "The Lord who delivered me from the paw of a lion and from the paw of a bear will deliver me from the hand of this Philistine!" was David's determined answer.

"Go, and the Lord be with you!" the despairing king blessed the eager youth.

Saul gave David his armor. He clothed him with a bronze helmet, a coat of mail and girded him with a heavy sword. David could barely move under the king's armor.

"I cannot wear these," he complained. "I am not used to them."

He took off the armor, and taking his staff in hand, he picked five smooth pebbles from the brook and put them in his shepherd's bag. With a sling in his other hand, he went to meet the Philistine giant.

When Goliath drew near and saw David, a mere youth, coming on to meet him, Goliath gave a loud bellow.

"Am I a dog that you come to meet me with sticks?" he ridiculed from a distance.

It was surely an insult for the Israelites to send a boy to challenge a mighty warrior, he thought. He cursed David by all his gods, despising him in great rage.

"Come to me and I will give your flesh to the birds of the air and to the beasts of the earth!" called the giant, gritting his teeth.

David retorted in a firm voice. "You come to me with sword, spear and javelin, but I come to you in the name of the Lord of hosts, God of the armies of Israel whom you have defied. This day I will slay you and cut off your head that all the earth may know that the Lord saves not with the sword and spear, for the battle is the Lord's and he will give you into our hands."

Goliath advanced and made ready for the fight. David, too, walked with quickened steps toward the battle line to meet the Philistine. Approaching his foe he took a stone from his bag and placed it in his sling. Stopping, he quickly measured the distance between himself and the huge man. He was like a mere ant in comparison to this collosal human. With one swift motion David aimed and fired the sling. The stone struck Goliath on the fore-

Goliath was armed with the coat of mail...

head between his eyes with such great force and violence that the great giant reeled and fell to the ground on his face.

David, rushing up to Goliath, drew the giant's sword from its sheath and cut off his head.

Upon seeing what happened, the king asked the commander of his army, "Abner, whose son is this youth?"

"As your soul lives, O king, I cannot tell," answered Abner.

"Then inquire whose son the stripling is!" commanded Saul.

Seeing their worst enemy smitten to the ground, the courage of the Israelites was revived. Running after the fleeing Philistines, they attacked them, taking over their possessions and their camps.

29. The Noble Friendship

Advancing with steady steps, holding in his one arm the dripping head of the Philistine and in the other hand his enemy's large sword, David approached the camp of Saul. From a distance Saul and his son Jonathan had watched the uneven match. There was something so noble and dignified in the young man's posture that it made Saul wonder.

When David climbed up the mountain Saul called for him and asked, "Young man, of what family are you?"

"I am the son of your servant Jesse, the Bethlehemite."

Prince Jonathan, standing next to his father, watched David with great admiration. In his youthful earnestness he saw in David a real hero. Scripture says:

> the soul of Jonathan was knit to the soul of David,
> and Saul took him that day, and would not let him
> return to his father's house. Then Jonathan made
> a covenant with David, because he loved him as
> his own soul.

Jonathan, Saul's oldest and favorite son, was also a favorite among soldiers and all Israelites. Scarcely older than David, he had distinguished himself in battle and was admired by his father's troops. Instead of being jealous, as one would naturally expect, Jonathan was one of those rare individuals who knew no envy and who could admire the triumphs of others without competitive feelings. Both David and Jonathan were intelligent, vivid, deep and sensitive youths. Their love for each other was mutual, complete and lasting, never overshadowed by jealousy.

Jonathan wanted David to be his friend forever, and they vowed loyalty to each other. On such occasions custom required friends to exchange their garments. Jonathan took his princely coat and gave it to David. He gave him his sword, his bow and his girdle. Adorned in princely clothes and armor, David had an air of royalty about him. This did not escape Saul's suspicious eye.

When the battle was over the royal cavalcade, with Saul, Jonathan at its head, returned home. Many people gathered on the streets and roadsides to hail their warriors and to express their joy for victory. The women came with flutes and cymbals, singing and dancing on the streets. There was a spontaneously sung song which echoed from one side of the street to another in joyful repetition:

Saul has slain his thousands,
and David his ten thousands.

Saul heard it. He listened more carefully, wondering if he had heard correctly. But the words rankled again and again until there was no mistaking — women on the streets were praising David more than him!

"What more can they do but make him king," he mused. "Am I not the ruler to whom belongs the praise and glory?" It was then that Saul's jealousy was born and from that moment on he regarded David as his rival.

After returning to camp, for Saul did not have a palace in which to live, he decided to get rid of David in an inconspicuous manner. He gave David men of war to fight the enemy, but after every battle David returned with a new victory and received even greater admiration from his people. David's popularity was surpassing the king's fame. Saul realized that the blessing of the Lord had left him. The more popular David became, the more depressed the king was.

One day when Saul was tormented by melancholy, he called David into his chamber to play for him on his harp. David played but the moody king was not pleased. He resisted the power of music to soothe him and complained that the songs bored him. David played the most beautiful tunes he knew, but they did not give joy to the king. Suddenly he drew his spear and hurled it at David, hoping to nail him to the wall. David jumped aside, avoiding the weapon.

Now more than ever Saul knew that the Lord was with David and that the Spirit of God had departed from himself. He was afraid of David and began seeking an opportunity to destroy him.

He made him captain over a thousand men and sent him to battle against an enemy outnumbering David's forces. Moreover, he promised to give his beautiful daughter in marriage if David himself would slay one hundred Philistines. To Saul's disappointment David returned having slain two hundred of the enemy, gaining the affection of the people of Israel. This enraged Saul even more.

Michal loved the good looking, brave David. She urged her father to give her in marriage as promised. In the back of his head Saul wanted Michal to spy on David. With this in mind, he consented to their marriage.

David's name was highly esteemed not only among his own people but even among his enemies. The more famous David became the more Saul despised him and, in jealous hatred, tried to put him away. Jonathan interceded for his friend but Saul would not listen even to his own beloved son. It was a difficult trial for Jonathan because he loved his father and he loved his friend.

Out of loyalty to his friendship Jonathan warned David, "My

father is seeking to kill you. Hide yourself in a secret place in a
field and I will come at night and tell you everything."

David listened to his friend's advice and remained hidden,
concealing himself in the fields, mountains and caves of the area.
Even as a fugitive David never lost confidence in God's protection.
Many of his beautiful songs known as "psalms" are preserved to
this day.

"Keep me safe, Lord. I put my trust in you," was the prayer
David repeated many times. While thinking about Jonathan he
sang:

> *"There are faithful souls in the land; wondrous*
> *delight it gives me in their companionship.*
>
> *"I bless the Lord who gives me counsel; in the night*
> *also my heart instructs me. I keep the Lord always*
> *before me; because he is at my right hand, I shall*
> *not be moved.*
>
> *"Hear a just cause, O Lord; attend to my cry!*
> *Give ear to my prayers from lips free of deceit!*
>
> *"Wondrously show thy steadfast love, O Saviour*
> *of those who seek refuge from their adversaries*
> *at thy right hand."*

One day when Saul was in a better mood Jonathan tried
again to reconcile King Saul with David.

"Sin not, O King, against your servant David because he has
not sinned against you." The king's favorite son then related to his
father all the good deeds that David had done while in the king's
service. "Why, therefore, will you sin against innocent blood?"
asked Jonathan with all the fervor of his soul.

The king was appeased by these words and swore that he
would not have David slain. Jonathan brought David back to his
father's presence. Saul was gracious to David as he was in the beginning of their acquaintance.

At this time war was renewed against the Philistines and

David went out to fight against them. He defeated them in splendid victory. When Saul saw that David's fame increased with every battle, he was again greatly disturbed and tried a second time
to pierce David with his spear while David played his harp. Once
again David eluded Saul's spear. With the help of his wife Michal
he escaped through their bedroom window and fled into hiding.

Saul's anger was even greater than before. Realizing that
David had escaped, he called Jonathan and ordered his son to find
David and kill him.

"As long as the son of Jesse lives upon this earth," said Saul,
"neither you nor your kingdom shall be established. Therefore
send and fetch him for he shall surely die."

"Why should he die? What has he done?" demanded Jonathan.

In answer Saul drew his spear to strike his son but the aging
king's arm was not as steady as it used to be. With the agility of
a young man, Jonathan warded off the blow and, fleeing from his
father, went to David's hiding place in Ramah.

In the darkness of night David waited for Jonathan, or at
least for some kind of message from him. When Jonathan arrived
at the appointed place David cried to him in despair, "What have
I done? What is my iniquity? There is but a step between me and
death!"

"I will do whatever your soul desires of me," swore Jonathan
to David.

Jonathan, knowing full well that there was no way for David
to return, continued speaking, "Go in peace. As for the oath both
of us have sworn in the name of the Lord, 'May the Lord be between me and you, and between my descendants and your descendants, forever.' "

The two friends embraced each other in a heartbreaking farewell. They were so close to each other, closer than two brothers.
Jonathan loved David as much as his soul would allow, and so
David loved Jonathan. The loyalty, beauty and nobility of their
friendship will always be remembered and referred to in human

history. It will encourage and inspire many hearts to open themselves and embrace true friendship.

Holy Scripture says "Nothing can be compared to a faithful
friend and they that fear the Lord shall find it." A true and noble
friendship is indeed a great gift to be cherished.

Troubled about the uncertainty of his future as a fugitive,
David was thankful to God for Jonathan. The two friends renewed
their vow of friendship in the name of God, and, weeping bitterly,
said goodbye to each other, parting forever.

Now David was all alone, cut off from everything and everyone he held dear. In his sorrow he turned to God in faith:

> *"The Lord lives; and blessed be my rock,*
> *and exalted be the God of my salvation,*
> *who delivered me from my enemies.*
> *Yea, thou didst exalt me above my adversaries;*
> *thou didst deliver me from the man of violence."*

But David was not delivered from "the man of violence," at
least not yet. Saul was still after David's life, and he was not safe
anywhere. He fled to the mountains of Judah. Being from the tribe
of Judah himself, he felt safer among his own people. But even
there death threatened him on every side.

In the Judean hills was the cave of Adullan, a great limestone
hollow in a mountain about ten miles from Bethlehem. David
knew it well. Years before as a shephed he had found shelter there.
Moving stealthily by night David reached the cave.

When David's father and brothers learned of his where-
abouts, they soon joined him. Some men in distress who were being persecuted by the king's guards joined David in twos and
threes. Before long there were about four hundred men — all
volunteers under David's leadership.

In order to protect his parents David sent them to the king
of Moab. They were welcomed there because David's grandmother
Ruth was a Moabite.

As soon as Saul heard where David was hiding he moved to

the nearby hills, taking three thousand men with him. David sent his spies to see where the king had pitched his tents. When the spies reported back to David, he arose and went secretly to the camp of his enemy. "Who will go down with me into the camp of Saul?" asked David of his men.

"I will go down with you," volunteered Abishai.

David and Abishai quietly entered the tents by night and found Saul sleeping on his cot, his spear fixed in the ground near his head. All the soldiers and his guard were asleep.

"I will run your enemy through with my spear, and there shall be no need of a second time," whispered eager Abishai.

"Kill him not," warned David, "for who shall put forth his hand against the Lord's anointed and remain guiltless? Take the spear and the cup of water and let us go."

No man saw or heard them as they entered and left the camp. Crossing the valley they climbed the opposite hill. There David shouted in a loud voice to Abner, the captain of Saul's army, "Will you not answer, Abner? Aren't you a man? Why didn't you guard your king?"

Hearing David's voice Saul woke up.

"Is that my son David?" cried the king.

"Yes, it is!" shouted David from the opposite hill. "Why do you persecute your servant? What have I done? May the Lord therefore judge between you and me."

At this moment Saul's spirit was enlightened and he cried out, "You are a more upright man than I for you have repaid me with good while I have repaid you with evil. May the Lord reward you. Now I know that you will rule Israel. Swear therefore that you will not cut off my seed after me, nor destroy my name from my father's house."

David gave Saul the oath of reassurance he begged for. Knowing full well how changeable the moods of the king were, he did not take another chance to go with him. There they parted in peace. David returned to his men and Saul went his way.

Meanwhile Samuel died, and all Israel mourned their prophet.

David had gathered around him a band of six hundred men, stalwart and ready to protect him. Of course six hundred men had to eat. Since David did not want to turn people against them, they were not permitted to take anything by force, only what people freely gave them.

There was a rich man named Nabal who was shearing sheep in Carmel. David sent ten of his young men to Nabal, asking him to give them food since David's men had protected Nabal's herds from attackers many times. Nabal, being churlish and ill-tempered, refused David's request. That irked David to anger and, taking four hundred men with him, he set on the road to get even with Nabal.

Not far from their encampment they met Nabal's wife Abigail who, hearing about her husband's foolishness, took matters into her own hands. She loaded a cart with food and, leading the donkey herself, went down the hill to meet David.

Beautiful and in the bloom of womanhood, Abigail stood in front of David apologizing for her husband's behavior and asking David to accept her offering. She looked at David with adoring eyes, seeing in him not only the legendary hero but also a very handsome man in the prime of his life. David accepted her offering and thanked her for sparing him from bloodshed.

When Nabal heard what Abigail did he became so enraged that in his temper outburst he had a stroke and died instantly, falling to the ground at Abigail's feet.

Ten days later, after Abigail buried her violent husband, David sent his men to ask her to become his wife. His first wife Michal was forcibly given away to another man, as one of Saul's revenges. This left David terribly lonely. With her heart full of willingness Abigail accepted the proposal.

Soon after that David took another wife Ahinoam.

After a short time the Philistines organized their forces to attack the Israelites. Not knowing what to do nor how to respond to the Philistines' demands, Saul engaged the prophets. He did not get any answer from them however. He himself did not have any prophetic dreams, and the Voice of God was silent. Upon seeing a great army of his enemy, Saul was afraid. In despair he disguised himself and went secretly to a witch to get counsel. Not too long before he had put to death all who practiced witchcraft, with the exception of one woman who was cunning enough to escape the snare of the king.

Saul asked the woman to call upon the spirit of Samuel to give him advice. The woman performed her witchery. The spirit of Samuel really appeared. All trembling with fear, his blood nearly froze in his veins. Saul listened to the message.

"Why have you disturbed me?" asked Samuel's spirit.

"I am in great distress!" cried Saul. "The Philistines are warring against me, and God has turned away from me."

"Why then do you ask me?" spoke the spirit. "Because you disobeyed the Voice of God he has taken your kingdom out of your hand and given it to David. Tomorrow you and your sons shall be with me. The Lord will give the army of Israel also into the hand of Philistines."

Hearing such a fatal prediction Saul fell prostrate on the ground. Only after the witch gave him some of her strong herbal brew did he slowly revive.

On the next day there was a battle between the Israelites and the Philistines on Mount Gilboa south of Naim. Saul fought together with his sons as a real soldier, disregarding the horrors of the night. A great number of Israelites were slain by the outnumbering Philistines. Three of Saul's sons combating side by side with their father, fell from enemy spears. Saul saw his beloved Jonathan die in a heroic duel with a huge Philistine. It was a complete defeat for the Israelites. Saul and his armor-bearer were left alone on the mountain top. By some strange predicament the enemy's weapons kept missing the king, although he did not try any more to avoid them. Saul saw that he was surrounded by the enemy and knew too well that if they captured him, they would make a cruel mockery of him. At last the king of Israel was grievously wounded by Philistine archers.

"Draw your sword and thrust it through me, lest the uncircumsized come and make sport of me!" he ordered his armor-bearer.

The armor-bearer who served his king loyally for many years could not do it. Therefore Saul took his own sword and fell upon it. Seeing that his master was dead the armor-bearer followed suit in the same manner.

It would seem that David was now delivered from his mortal enemy and that he should rejoice. But nothing could be farther from that. When he heard the news he wept bitterly forgetting all the injuries he had received and remembering only the good qualities of the king. Filled with sorrow David rent his garments and put on the sack of a mourner. He lamented over Saul's death and, in deep grief, he lamented the death of his loyal friend Jonathan.

Thy glory, O Israel, is slain upon thy high places!
How are the mighty fallen!
Tell it not in Gath,
publish it not in the streets of Ashkelon;
lest the daughters of uncircumcized exult.

Ye mountains of Gilboa,
let there be no dew or rain upon you,
nor upsurging of the deep!
For there the shield of the mighty was defiled,
the shield of Saul, not anointed with oil.

Saul and Jonathan, beloved and lovely!
In life and in death they were not divided;
they were swifter than eagles,
they were stronger than lions.

Ye daughters of Israel weep over Saul,
who clothed you daintily in scarlet,
who put ornaments of gold upon your apparel!

Jonathan lies slain upon thy high places.
I am distressed for you, my brother Jonathan;

very pleasant have you been to me;
your love to me was wonderful,
passing the love of women.

How are the mighty fallen,
and the weapons of war perished!

30. King David

(Circa 1000 B.C.)

After the death of Saul, David was proclaimed king, but not without bloodshed. One of Saul's sons, the young Ishbosheth, was immediately anointed king of the northern part of the kingdom. On his side was Abner, Saul's able army commander. David patiently waited for seven years until the power of the young inexperienced king came to an end. Abner, seeing the disintegration of the Northern Kingdom, left Ishbosheth to his own fate and joined David. But not for long. Soon he was killed by his rivals without David's consent. King Ishbosheth was murdered in his sleep by two men. This murder was also done without David's knowledge, by the conspirators seeking King David's favor.

David was the king "according to God's own heart." He deserved this name because of his deep reverence and openness to divine revelations and inspirations. Humbly he realized that the authority of the king came from God, not from the people. Being a fugitive from the rage of Saul for a long time, he learned to value God's friendship. Out of reverence he spared Saul's life, even endangering his own, because Saul was the anointed of the Lord.

During his reign David united and enlarged the kingdom, drove the Jebusites out of Jerusalem, formed the priestly tribe of Levites into choirs, wrote psalms for divine worship and above all honored the Ark of the Covenant. David proved to be a great king, a great mystic and a great poet. His psalms, although now 3000 years old, are still considered among the best poetry ever written.

In the beginning of his reign David first of all established his court in Jerusalem. Jerusalem or Jeru-Salem means the House of Peace. Earlier it was called Salem from which in the days of Abraham came the king and high priest Melchisedek. When David was elevated to the throne the town was divided into two parts: the lower part belonged to the Israelites; but the strongly fortified upper town on Mt. Sion belonged to the Jebusites.

In a most daring battle David took possession of Mt. Sion and fortified it even more strongly. With forced labor, used for the first time in Hebrew history by another Hebrew, he built himself a palace there and called it the City of David. From then on Jerusalem instead of Hebron was considered the capital of the kingdom and the religious center of Israel.

On Mt. Sion David erected a new Tabernacle for the Ark of the Covenant. When the Tabernacle was completed the Ark of the Covenant was brought up in solemn procession to the new capital. David celebrated the victory with music, singing and dancing. He became so intoxicated with jubilation that he gave himself up to ecstasy, dancing, singing and leaping at the head of the joyous procession. He danced before the Lord, singing this song of exultation:

Lift up your heads, O gates!
and be lifted up, O ancient doors!
that the King of glory may come in.

Who is the King of glory?
The Lord strong and mighty,
the Lord, mighty in battle!

Who will bring me to the fortified city?

Be exulted, O God, above the heavens!
Let thy glory be over all the earth!
Grant us help against the foe,
for vain is the help of man!
With God we shall do valiantly;
it is he who will tread down our foes.

Watching the procession from the upper window of the palace Michal, Saul's daughter whom David lost and regained again through some political maneuvers, was quite disturbed with the king's behavior. It was not to her liking. She despised her common born husband for behaving like a peasant publicly degrading his royal dignity. When the procession came to an end David offered burnt sacrifices and peace offerings at the new Tabernacle. He blessed the people in the name of the Lord and distributed bread, cakes and meat. The whole city was in a high spirit of celebration.

In an elated mood David returned home to bless his household. Michal came to meet him feeling scorn that David had lost his dignity mixing and dancing like a common fool before the people. This scorn was like a sting to David. As emotional as he tended to be, he was deeply wounded that his wife did not understand him.

"I was before the Lord," was his excruciating answer. "And I will make merry before the Lord. I will make myself yet more contemptible than this and I will be abased in your eyes, but honored in the sight of my people."

David and Michal on that day became like two strangers. He never entered her chamber again, and she had no more children.

Using the cedars of Lebanon David built himself a beautiful house. It was a palace with many rooms for his numerous wives, children and concubines. One day an inspiring thought came to David who was always active and creative.

"Look, I live in a beautiful house," he mused to himself as if in regret, while my Lord lives in a tent. I shall build HIM a house more beautiful than any man has seen!"

He gathered around himself the most famous architects and artisans from near and far. Together with them in great excitement he studied plans and drawings for a temple that would give the greatest glory to God. He was eager to start his project, but one unpredicted delay followed another. David became frustrated. He was an absolute monarch who ruled with power, demanding all the loyalty and obedience of his citizens. But everything seemed to work against him, even nature.

At that time an old man came to his palace. He was clothed in a dusty grey robe, his long hair and beard white as snow. Although aged and lean he had an air of authority about his posture and his unusually strong voice. He demanded an immediate audience with the king. Soon David learned his name was Nathan, which means "God Gives." He came to counsel David, a daring proposition to the man of might. Intuitively David knew that God was speaking through this prophet and before long he started to depend on Nathan's guidance.

One day Nathan told King David to give up the idea of building a temple. "Give up? The old man must be out of his mind," thought David. If there was anything at all that David really wanted in his life, it was a magnificent temple, a dwelling place for his beloved Lord, who had protected him and had given him so much. Why shouldn't he build this wonderous monument?

Nathan's straightforward answer was astonishing to David:

> *"Thus says the Lord of hosts: Would you build me a house. When your days are fulfilled and you lie down with your fathers, I will raise up your offspring after you, who shall come forth from your body, and I will establish his kingdom. He shall build a house for my name and I will establish the throne of his kingdom for ever."*

This prophecy wasn't all. David knew it. He read it right in Nathan's face. With the diplomacy that David had, he soon found out from the old man the whole truth. Who was David to build the Temple to the Lord? He, whose hands were stained with the blood of many battles, who had killed hundreds with his own hands—who was he to build a dwelling place to the Lord?

David bowed his head. If this is what the Lord wants, let it be. There was the promise the Lord gave: a son of David would build a Temple.

David accepted the predicament with royal grace and humble submission to the will of God. If his son would build the Temple and not him, then at least he would provide the materials for the

tremendous undertaking. He not only provided cedar, marble, gold
and other building materials, he also wrote words and music to be
sung in the Temple. He organized a choir of one thousand singers,
with two hundred and eighty teachers of music.

There was a very tender relationship between Yahweh and
David, one of father to son. When a son does something wrong,
the father punishes him.

*"I will be his father and he shall be my son. When he
does wrong I will punish him as any father might,
and not spare a rod."*

In loving submission David thanked the Lord. That day he
made a firm resolution to do only what was right and just in the
Lord's eyes.

31. Bathsheba

David was officially proclaimed king when he was thirty years
old. Ten years passed from that time in a regular everyday routine.
The flame of his first love Michal withered gradually. Then it died
completely when David was confronted with Michal's hatred toward him. Although David had many wives, as well as power and
wealth, his heart felt empty. The king-poet suffered from the bore-
dom of middle age. All the glory around him, nor his achieve-
ments gave him enough excitement. David felt empty and restless.

On evenings, after a hot day, he would go up to the roof-top
in the refreshing breeze, and walk there alone with his thoughts
aimlessly wandering hither and thither. One evening while pacing
back and forth his eyes caught a neighboring woman taking a bath.
David stood there watching her as though taken by surprise. The
woman was beautifully shaped and being unaware that she was
being watched, she just continued to wash herself. Observing her
graceful movements David was flooded with emotions he had not
known for years. He was instantly infatuated. His heart burned
with desire, he wanted this woman. Calling his servant he asked
who she was but the servant did not know either.

"Then go and find out," was the king's request.

Soon the servant returned telling him that she was named Bathsheba, the wife of Uriah the Hittite.

"Bring her to me," commanded David.

Two of the king's servants went to summon beautiful Bathsheba. A sudden call from a king, especially such an urgent one, could mean many things. Bathsheba was not given time even to braid her long damp hair nor to pin it up. Worried why she was being summoned, she wrapped herself in a long veil and followed the two men to the king's palace.

King David, a fierce lion in battle but most affectionate and gentle in love, was impatiently waiting for Bathsheba. When she was brought in he saw that her beauty surpassed every woman he had ever met. Trembling in front of the mighty king, Bathsheba fell on her knees, but King David raised her up. Before she could utter a single word, he embraced her and sealed her lips with his.

Not until three nights later did Bathsheba leave the king's chambers to go home. Before long she sent a message to the king, "I am with child." In those days the news would fill any woman with happiness, but in Bathsheba's circumstances it filled her with anguish and fear. Uriah the Hittite, her husband, was at the battlefield with David's trustworthy general Joab. David sent word to Joab to send Uriah home on vacation, hoping Uriah would spend time with Bathsheba and later assume that her child by David was his own. He did not go to his wife, but stayed in the barracks with other soldiers. David tried to wheedle him into going to his wife. He even offered him wine and fine food and tried to bribe him with presents and flattery.

David loved Bathsheba more than any woman. His flame for her was so devastating that he decided to put away the stubborn Hittite. Back to the battlefield he had to go with a letter to Joab in his pocket: "Set Uriah in the forefront that he may be struck down and die."

The order was obeyed. Uriah was killed in action and as soon as the customary mourning period was over there was a splendid

wedding ceremony in which Bathsheba became not only King
David's wife but also a queen.

Gossip, especially from David's numerous jealous wives, was
spreading—first in Jerusalem, then over all Israel. Everyone knew,
Bathsheba was with child before they were married. A son was
born shortly after their wedding. The king loved the boy and
adored his wife. People everywhere were whispering to each other:
"How long will the Lord God be silent?"

Out of his cave scampered old Nathan. With a staff much
taller than himself, he climbed the steep dusty road to Mount
Sion, heading for the palace. Ragged and worn out he stood in
front of the great king. It seemed in the beginning that he had
come for a peaceful and friendly chat with the king. He did not
accuse him of anything. He set a trap for David, telling this story:
A certain rich man, who had large herds of sheep, made a feast
for a traveler. Instead of killing one of his own fatlings, he took
his poor neighbor's only ewe to prepare the feast.

Hearing of such an injustice David was moved with anger.

"The man shall surely die," was the king's judgment. "And he
shall restore the lamb fourfold, because he did this thing, and because he had no pity."

"You are the man," said Nathan sternly. "You have smitten
Uriah with the sword and have taken his wife."

"I have sinned against the Lord," admitted David.

His response to Nathan reveals the greatness of his soul.
David confessed that his sin was a great one and he genuinely repented for offending God.

"The Lord has put away your sin; you shall not die," spoke
the prophet. "Nevertheless, because by this deed you have utterly
scorned the Lord, the child that is born to you shall die."

Nathan left. That same night the child became restless with
fever. David humbled himself before God and prayed for the life
of his son. For seven days the child was in agony of death, and
David in agony of soul. He fasted and prayed laying on the ground,
weeping and lamenting. He poured out his suffering into one of
his most profound psalms:

> *"Have mercy on me, O God, according to thy stead-*
> *fast love; according to thy abundant mercy blot out*
> *my transgressions. Wash me thoroughly from my*
> *iniquity, and cleanse me from my sin!*
> *For I know my transgressions and my sin is ever*
> *before me.*
> *Against thee, thee only, have I sinned, and done*
> *which is evil in thy sight,*
> *so that thou art justified in thy sentence and blame-*
> *less in thy judgment.*
> *Behold, I was brought forth in iniquity, and in sin*
> *did my mother conceive me.*
> *Behold, thou desirest truth in the inward being;*
> *thence teach me wisdom in my secret heart . . .*
> *Create in me a clean heart, O God, and put a new*
> *and right spirit within me.*
> *Cast me not away from thy presence, and take not*
> *thy holy spirit from me.*
> *Restore to me the joy of thy salvation,*
> *and uphold me with a willing spirit.*
> *Then I will teach transgressors thy ways,*
> *and sinners will return to thee.*
> *Deliver me from bloodguiltiness, O God,*
> *Thou God of my salvation,*
> *and my tongue will sing aloud of thy deliverance."*

With every day David's son grew weaker. On the evening of
the seventh day David noticed the servants whispering. They were
afraid to confront their king with the truth, for fear he might do
harm to himself. But David was a more practical man than his
servants thought him to be.

"Is the child dead?" asked the king.

"He is dead."

David arose, washed, anointed himself and went to the house
of the Lord to worship. When the surprised servants asked why
he changed so suddenly, David answered, "Can I bring him back

again? I shall go to him, but he will not return to me." He prayed
for the child's life, but when the child was dead he did not waste
any time. He regarded this as divine justice at work.

David comforted Bathsheba. The suffering they both experienced deepened their love, uniting them closer to each other.
When Bathsheba knew that God had blessed her again, joy and
confidence returned to her heart. She bore a son and they called
him Solomon, which means "Peace." From the moment of birth
this child showed unusual alertness. David loved his new-born son
and his son's beautiful mother with such intensity that he vowed
to her, leaning over the child's crib, "Solomon will be the king!"
There were many other sons born before this child who could
claim their birthright to the throne.

32. Absalom — the Rebelling Son

When David confessed, God told him through Nathan that
his sin was forgiven, but this still did not mean that he would be
free from chastisement. It came soon, through his older son Absalom whom David dearly loved. Absalom's grandfather, on his
mother's side, was king of Geshur, and Absalom was proud of his
royal blood. He was an extremely handsome youth but he was
also just as cunning. The Holy Scripture says:

> Now in all Israel there was no one so much praised
> for his beauty as Absalom; from the sole of his foot
> to the crown of his head there was no blemish on
> him.

Absalom had long beautiful hair, and all his bearing had dignity and attraction. David gave Absalom a princely retinue of
chariots and horsemen, and a guard of young men to accompany
him everywhere. But what was hidden to all was not a secret to
Absalom's mother Talmai. With a woman's intuition she knew why
her son was not trained for stately affairs, but rather raised to be

only a "prince charming." She decided to help her son climb to the throne. It was she who gave Absalom instructions on how to plot against his own father.

Absalom was an early riser. Before the day started he stationed himself at the palace gate. When any man presented himself to ask justice of the king, he kindly inquired what complaint he had to make. Upon hearing it he always replied: "Thy words seem good and just to me, but there is no one appointed by the king to hear the cause." In this manner he made friends for himself among people and created dissatisfaction with the king.

Sometimes he would exclaim in hearing these people, "O, that they would make me judge over the land, that all who have business might come to me, that I may do them justice!" Moreover, when any man saluted him, he would go to that man, embrace him and kiss him. In this manner, by flattery and throwing bad light on his father, he enticed the hearts of Israelites. When he thought he had gained enough popularity and that a great number of men were on his side, he asked his father to let him go to Hebron in fulfillment of a vow. David, suspecting no evil, did not object.

Reaching Hebron Absalom sent out messengers to all the tribes of Israel, telling them that when they heard the sound of a trumpet they should say, "Absalom is king at Hebron." Not knowing his treachery many people followed Absalom. Even David's counselor was with him.

When David heard about Absalom's revolt, although it was a shocking surprise to him, his love toward his son did not turn into anger. David decided to leave the city instead of fighting his own son and creating a civil war with the bloodshed of his own people.

In front of the sad train went his wives, children and all the people who willingly followed him. The Levites came with their high priest Zadok carrying the Ark of the Covenant of God. David waited until all the people passed, then he said to Zadok, "Carry the Ark of God back into the city. If I find favor in the eyes of the Lord, he will bring me back."

Barefoot and his head veiled with a sack as a humble peni-
tent, David crossed a brook in the Valley of Kedron and came to
the Mount of Olives. There he wept for his son's transgressions
and his own sins. On the same mountain years later Christ was to
know the agony of Gethsemane for the sins of mankind.

On the side of the Mount of Olives David was met by a man
from the family of Saul named Shimei, who threw stones and dirt
at David and cursed him. Abishai, the king's attendant, was upset
about it and said to David, "Why should this dead dog curse the
king? Let me go over and take off his head!"

"Behold, my own son seeks my life," the king answered sadly.
"How much more strongly must this Benjamite feel. Let him alone
and let him curse, for the Lord has bidden him. It may be that
the Lord will look upon my affliction, and that the Lord will repay
me with good for his cursing of me today."

He saw the hand of God in this trial and he calmly continued
his weary journey toward the Jordan River.

Absalom's goal was obvious—the throne. To reach it there
was just one way: to destroy the reigning king, his father. With
his men he pursued King David to the Jordan River.

After a short rest on the banks of the Jordan, David organized
his men to resist the attackers. He wanted to go into battle himself, but when his men did not permit him to do it, he ordered
Joab, his genius commander, to lead the battle. Before leaving,
David blessed his men and said to Joab and his officers, "For my
sake deal gently with the young man Absalom!"

The battle was fought in the midst of a great forest, and Absalom's army was defeated and scattered. Absalom mounted a
mule in an attempt to escape through the forest. As he rushed
away, galloping and beating his mule, his long hair caught in the
branches of an oak tree. His hair entangled in a tree. Absalom
dangled helplessly on a swaying branch while his mule passed on.
David's soldiers saw the prisoner and sent a message to Joab, the
commander.

"Why did you not smite him to the ground?" Joab yelled angrily, rushing to the tree entangling Absalom. "I will not waste time like this with you." He took three darts in his hand and thrust them into the heart of Absalom. He was still alive when ten young men, Joab's armor bearers, surrounded him, struck him and killed him. They put Absalom's body in a pit and piled a large heap of stones over it.

A herald with news of Absalom's defeat was sent to David.

"Is Absalom safe?" David asked with the anxiety of a father. Learning the truth the king did not rejoice over the victory. He went up to a chamber over the camp gate, closed the door behind him and wept.

"O my son Absalom, my son, my son!"

There was no one who could console David. For weeks he remained indoors lamenting and composing psalms of his grief. No other trial, his many years as Saul's fugitive nor the many dangerous battles, could compare to the loss of his loved son Absalom.

At last Joab, his sister's son and a chief-commander of the army, grew impatient. Was this young revolter more precious to the king than all the soldiers who fought for him, or all his subjects whom he had neglected for such a long time? Joab went to see the king and to reason with him.

"Arise, go out and speak kindly to your servants," Joab urged him. "Or this will be worse for you than all the evil that has come upon you."

Being not only a poet but also a man of common sense, David knew exactly when to stop and attend to matters. He changed his mourning garments for the royal robe and took his seat in front of the city gate. News about the king's appearance spread faster than wild fire. People from all directions flowed to the city gates to greet their ruler. In a brief speech the king addressed his subjects. When he finished speaking someone in the crowd called, "Why don't we bring our king back?"

Hearing the call many voices reechoed: "Back to Jerusalem! Return, O king, to Jerusalem!"

King David was carried by the men of Juda in a triumphant procession from Bethlehem back to Mount Sion, to the City of David.

33. King David's Sunset Years

David ruled and judged Israel for forty years. There were many wars he fought, never losing a single battle, because the Lord of hosts was on his side. Even after returning from his last exile and after three years of peace, he had to enter another war with the Philistines. When the war was over and the troops returned home, David composed songs again.

> *And David spoke to the Lord the words of this song on the day when the Lord delivered him from the hand of all his enemies*
>
> *The Lord is my rock, and my fortress, and my deliverer. . . .*
> *I call upon the Lord, who is worthy to be praised, and I am saved from my enemies.*
>
> *The Lord rewarded me according to my righteousness;*
> *according to the cleanness of my hands he recompensed me.*
>
> *The spirit of the Lord speaks by me, his word is upon my tongue.*

It was obvious that God blessed David and not only favored all his undertakings but also promised him that one of his descendants would rule the whole world and sit upon an everlasting throne. David had a gift of prophecy in which he expressed the eternal relationship between the Father and the Son: "Thou art my Son, this day I have begotten thee."
He foretold the future happenings in the ruling of the next

king, his son, how the kings of different nations would bring offerings to him and that he would be called the "Prince of Peace." He foretold the more distant future, almost one thousand years distant, the crucifixion with all its sorrowful details: "They have pierced my hands and feet, I count all my bones — they stare and gloat over me; they divide my garments among them, and for my raiment they cast lots." (Ps. 22)

> *"They gave me gall to eat,*
> *and for my thirst they gave me vinegar to drink."*
> *(Ps. 69)*

David wrote many songs expressing the anguish of his soul, especially during the flight from Saul and the revolt of his son Absalom. In many of these psalms the Holy Spirit had guided his thoughts, so that he expressed the feelings of His Son, the suffering Messiah on the Cross.

"My God, my God, why have you foresaken me?" was the cry of Jesus on the Cross quoted in David's psalm. It is possible, that in his mind Christ was continuing David's prayer:

> *"Loudly I call, but my prayer can not reach you.*
> *You do not answer, my God, when I cry out to you*
> *day and night, you do not heed."*

The last words on the Cross spoken by Jesus were taken from David's Psalm 30. As Christ hung dying on the Cross, with his last breath he whispered the words of the prayer which David wrote ten centuries beforehand: "Father, into your hands I commend my spirit." It is quite likely that Christ had been praying with the words of the psalmist during the three hours while hanging on the Cross. The entire Psalm 30 describes Christ's passion.

David, the forefather of Jesus—Jesus called himself the Son of David—seems to be so closely related to Christ. David, just like Jesus, was born in Bethlehem. He had a lowly birth and an obscure childhood. His victories over the enemies and the fact that he was also a king and a prophet, made the similarities even greater.

After three peaceful years, since David's return to Jerusalem, another famine was spreading its deadly fingers over Israel. The common belief was that someone, somewhere, was responsible for the plague. David in an attempt to appease God (or his murmuring subjects!) decided to exterminate all of Saul's family, every member. Another bloodshed started. All "subversive" subjects were hung on a hilltop outside Jerusalem.

David, as long as the history of mankind is written and read, will be remembered as a great king. The glory of Israel was never so great as it was in his time, for he built a strong and prosperous nation. He was aging now, he was "old and advanced in years."

Nights in Jerusalem are very chilly, and the king was shivering from the cold. The servants tried to cover him up with warm blankets but the blood in the king's veins was chilling and he could not warm up. The king's attendants decided to get a young girl to wait on the king, so that his blood would warm up. They found a very beautiful maiden named Shunamite and brought her to the king. She served the aged king, but to be his wife — "the king knew her not."

While David warmed his heart gazing at young Shunamite and mostly lived in his dreams of the glorious past, the matters of state were not attended to. One of David's sons, Adonijah, decided that his father was too old and senile to rule the kingdom. Gathering chariots and friends he left the city and threw a big feast in the country. When the gaiety reached its highest point he proclaimed: "I will be king!"

In their company was Joab and the priest Abiathar, two of the most important figures in the state, and everything seemed to be settled. A gay and wine-intoxicated party acclaimed the new king.

Meanwhile out of his cave came the old prophet Nathan, who was not invited to the party and made his way straight to the king's palace. Realizing that there was no sense for him to reason with the aging king who lived in the oblivion of his dreams, he first met secretly with Bathsheba, mother of Solomon. Although physically weak and weary from old age and a rigorous life, Nathan was still strong and determined in his spirit. This was the last task he had to perform as David's spiritual guide. After that he could rest with his forefathers.

"Have you not heard that Adonijah, the son of Haggith, has become king and that David does not know about it?" he asked Bathsheba.

Instructed by Nathan, Bathsheba went to see the king. Surprised at her entrance David asked, "What is it that you want?"

Bathsheba reminded the king how he swore to her a long time ago that Solomon would reign after him. She explained that now, without the king's blessing Adonijah had proclaimed himself king. At that moment Nathan entered the room. David always had great respect for Nathan and seeing him at this moment, he took it as sign from God.

"Solomon your son shall reign after me and he shall sit upon the throne," declared King David to Bathsheba, giving orders to Nathan and priest Zadok to anoint Solomon immediately as the new king.

As soon as Solomon was anointed the trumpets were blown to proclaim the great news.

"Long live King Solomon!" people were calling everywhere. The noise reached even the merrymakers of Adonijah's party.

"What is all that noise about in the city?" they asked each other. Soon people came to them bringing the news. The members of the party scattered. Adonijah, filled with fear, ran to the tent of the Lord and taking the horns of the altar blew for God's protection. The first act of King Solomon was mercy: he told Adonijah to go home.

With every day David grew weaker. On his deathbed he charged Solomon, "I am about to go the way of all on earth, be strong and show yourself a man. Keep the charge of the Lord your God, walking in his ways."

David, the greatest king on earth, a great poet and lover of God, died peacefully and was buried on Mount Sion in the City of David.

34. Solomon — the King of Peace

Once David said to his son Solomon, "Serve God with a perfect heart; for the Lord searches all the hearts and thoughts of the soul."

Solomon contemplated these words when he ascended to the throne. He was a very young and inexperienced king to rule such a contradictory nation, and he fully realized it. Like his father David, he loved the Lord and soon after his enthronement he went to Gibeon, the ancient highplace for sacrifice. There he offered burnt offerings upon the altar.

When the offerings were mere coal still glowing under the ashes in the dark of night, Solomon, like Jacob, had a prophetic dream. The Lord God looked with compassion on the youthful king and spoke to him in loving gentleness.

"Ask what you will that I should give you," spoke the Voice of the Lord in Solomon's dream.

Such unexpected kindness was surely a surprise to the son of David. Even in his dream Solomon weighed his answer slowly, taking hold of all his humility and his father's piety.

> *"Thou hast shown great and steadfast love to thy servant David my father because he walked before thee in faithfulness, in righteousness and in uprightness of heart toward thee; and thou hast kept for him this great and steadfast love, and hast given him a son to sit on his throne this day. Now, O Lord my God, thou has made thy servant king in place of David my father although I am but a mere child. I do not know how to go out or come in. Thy servant is in the midst of thy people whom thou hast chosen, a great people, that cannot be numbered or counted for multitude. Give thy servant therefore an understanding mind to govern thy people, that I may discern between good and evil; for who is able to govern this thy great people?"*

For such a plea the Lord God was greatly pleased. Was it Solomon's willing heart to serve God, or his humility? In him was fulfilled the proverb: "To the meek God will give grace."

"Because you have asked this, and have not asked for yourself long life or riches, behold, I now do according to your word. I will give you a wise and discerning mind, so that none like you has been before you and none like you shall arise after you. I give you also what you have not asked, both riches and honor, so that no other king shall compare with you, all your days. And if you will walk in my ways, keeping my statutes and my commandments, as your father David walked, then I will lengthen your days."

Solomon awoke. Although it was a dream, there was no doubt, the Lord himself had spoken in it. This gave the twenty-year-old king an air of assurance. That night the boy became a man. Tall, handsome and confident Solomon returned to Jerusalem watched with awe by his surprised courtiers.

Once in Jerusalem Solomon ordered a great feast. He stood before the Ark of the Covenant and offered up burnt sacrifices and peace offerings.

Right after the feast Solomon was confronted with a problem at which his wisdom as a judge was put to test. Two harlots came to seek the king's decision in their argument. Both women had children at about the same time and both lived in the same room. One woman accidently overlaid her child while in sleep and it died. Rising in the dark of night she exchanged the dead child for another woman's living child.

"When I arose in the morning," said the accusing woman, "Behold, my child was dead. But considering him closely, I found it was not mine."

"It is not as you say," argued the other woman holding the living child. "Your child is dead and not mine."

So they argued back and forth before the king. Then Solomon ordered that a swordsman be brought before him.

"Divide the living child in two and give half to one and half to the other," spoke the king.

Hearing this, the woman whose child was alive cried in terror, "I beseech you, my lord, give her the child alive, and do not kill it."

While the other said, "Let it be neither thine nor mine, but divide it."

Solomon heard it and knew immediately who was the real mother. He gave the child to her. After a few more similar decisions Solomon became renowned for his wisdom. People from all over the hills and valleys came to him for advice or to settle their disputes. Solomon's name in Hebrew means "Peaceful" and in history he is known as a peaceful king. Instead of making wars he made marriage alliances with his neighbors, that way cultivating friendly relations between kingships.

His first marriage alliance was with Pharaoh's daughter, an Egyptian princess. This marriage proved to be a great success in every way. First of all Egypt was a very powerful neighbor, well-armed and the most advanced nation in art, science and architecture.

The Egyptian princess' name is not mentioned in the Bible, apparently because she was a foreigner and marriages between foreigners, according to the law of Moses, were not accepted. She was a very beautiful and intelligent person. In Pharaoh's court and temple she was well-educated not only in their deities and religious customs, but also in art, literature and social refinement. Solomon loved her.

While on a stately visit to Egypt he was dazzled by the Egyptian splendor, their architecture, their ceremonial processions and pomp. He was impressed with their art and vast knowledge and he yearned to surpass every king on earth in splendor. He wanted to provide his adored bride with all the luxury she had in her father's palace and even more. This woman, "dark but beautiful," proved to be in years to come his favorite wife among all the oth-

"Divide the living child in two," spoke the king.

ers he accumulated. He built a separate palace in Jerusalem for her.

The Egyptian princess brought with her a large dowry and considerably enriched the state. This was to Solomon's liking, and he decided to do it again with many of his neighbors; he married their royal daughters making Israel more and more prosperous and a land of peace. Every marriage was followed by a great wedding feast, an affair of state, with a holiday for the people. The whole nation prospered. Solomon's glory was spreading beyond the borders of Israel.

King Solomon was a brilliant organizer with the mind of a genius. He divided the land into twelve districts with a chosen deputy in each. The people—with exception of the tribe of Judah from whom Solomon came — were heavily taxed. Each deputy had to provide the king and his palace for one month a year with food, clothing and everything that his enormous family and army of servants needed. For his own use Solomon had fourteen hundred chariots, twelve thousand horsemen and forty thousand stalls for horses.

In the fourth year of his reign Solomon began to build the Temple of the Lord on Mount Moria, on which Abraham once had set an altar in preparation to sacrifice his son Isaac. Mount Moria is to the southeast of Mount Sinai with a valley in-between. He had ten thousand men cutting cedars on Mount Lebanon, and seventy thousand were carrying materials to the site of the temple. Eighty thousand were hewing stones in the quarries, while three thousand three hundred were employed as overseers of the work with chief architect Hiram, the king of Tire, whom David had employed to build his palace.

"King Solomon raised a levy of forced labor out of Israel. . ." The house was built of stones hewed and made ready in the quarries so that neither hammer nor any other tool was heard in the Temple. It took more than seven years to build the structure. It was a rectangle, about one hundred and four feet long and about thirty feet wide, with its height equal to its width. Inside the Tem-

ple there were three parts: the porch, the sanctuary and the Holy
of Holies. The Holy of Holies was made a perfect cube, with the
veil in front of the door—it was the resting place for the Ark of the
Covenant in which were reposing the two stone tablets of the law,
guarded by two cherubim angels with outstretched wings plated
with pure gold.

Solomon found Hiram, the Phoenician architect, an enthusiastic creator. The two genius minds worked together with ardent
joy. The Temple was a real marvel not only outside but also inside. All the furniture was of purest gold. The walls of the Holy of
Holies were covered with plates of pure gold.

The Temple was finished about 970 B.C. It was a wonder to
the whole world and a crown of glory to Israel. Israel blossomed
as never before in a golden age of peace and prosperity. For the
first time in their history they could plow their land without fear,
sleep peacefully under olive and fig trees and plan for their future.
Their basic needs satisfied, Israelites turned their minds to cultural
matters, literature, art and music.

> *And God gave Solomon depth of wisdom and
> insight, and understanding as wide as sand on the
> seashore, so that Solomon's wisdom surpassed that
> of all the men of the East and all Egypt. For he
> was wiser than any man; his fame spread among all
> the surrounding nations. He uttered three thousand
> proverbs, and his songs numbered a thousand and
> five. Men from all races came to listen to the wis-
> dom of Solomon, and from all the kings of the earth
> who had heard of his wisdom he received gifts.*

At this time old stories and sagas were collected and written
into the first five books of the Bible. It was the first comprehensive
account of Israel's history put into writing. Being always on the
lookout not to lose their faith "Yahvist" of "J", as they called
themselves, gathered together the old traditions into one dramatically written document which showed God's steadfast love for Is-

rael. This document, outliving all the temples and palaces, always increased in popularity.

When the Temple of God was finished, although there is a legend that the interior was never finished, it stood like a gem in the azure sky of Jerusalem on top of Mount Moria. The time to dedicate the Temple was on hand. The words of dedication are preserved until this day, while the Temple itself was to pass away after four centuries.

The day of dedication coincided with the New Year Feast. The elders, the chiefs of the Israel tribes, arrayed in gorgeous robes, led by priests carrying the Ark of the Covenant, proceeded in solemn procession from Mount Sion to Mount Moria, with worshipping people gathered in great multitude on the roadsides.

When the Ark was placed in the Holy of Holies a cloud of fog filled the inner Temple and the assembled people cried that this must be the glory of the Lord, who not only approved his new dwelling place, but came down himself in a tangible way to dwell in it.

Solomon watched the happening in awe and joy. Filled with the Spirit of God he stood up to address his subjects:

> *"The Lord has set the sun in the heavens,*
> *but has said he would dwell in thick darkness,*
> *I have built thee an exalted house, a place*
> *for thee to dwell in forever."*

His hands stretched out toward heaven blessing the congregation, and with it the whole of Israel, he continued:

> *O Lord, God of Israel, there is no God like thee,*
> *in heaven above or on the earth beneath,*
> *keeping covenant and showing steadfast love*
> *to thy servants who walk before thee*
> *with all their heart.*
> *Now, O Lord, God of Israel, keep with thy servant*
> *David my father what thou hast promised him,*
> *saying, "There shall never fail you a man before me*

to sit upon the throne of Israel, if only your sons
take heed to their way, to walk before me."

"But will God indeed dwell on earth?
Behold the heaven of heavens can not contain you,
how much less this house which I have built!"

The dedication of the Temple was a most magnificent feast.
Immense sacrifices were offered on the new altars of the Temple:
220,000 oxen and 120,000 sheep were slaughtered and burned in
the seven day ceremonials. The jubilation of the Israelites was a
sheer ecstacy. In a dramatically concrete way the Temple was
proof of the presence of the living God among his people.

Solomon and the Israelites knew too well that God cannot be
put in a box to live. That is why Solomon asked, "But will God
indeed dwell on earth?"

The answer to this came in the prayer Solomon uttered:

"O Lord God, hearkening to the cry and to the
prayer which thy servant prays before thee this day,
that thy eyes may be open night and day toward
this house, the place of which thou said, 'My name
shall be there.'"

The feasts over, tired but elated in spirit, the people returned
to their homes. Solomon's humble prayer was pleasing to God.
He spoke to him a second time. Solomon knew it was the same
voice that spoke to him in a dream on Mount Gibeon.

"I have heard your prayer and your supplication, I
have consecrated this house which you have built
and put my name there forever; my eyes and my
heart will be there for all time. And as for you, if
you will walk before me, as David your father
walked, with integrity of heart and uprightness, do-
ing according to all I have commanded you, then I
will establish your royal throne over Israel forever,
as I promised David your father. But if you turn

aside, you or your children, and do not keep my commandments, but go and serve other gods and worship them, then I will cut off Israel from the land which I have given them, and the house which I have consecrated for my name I will cast out of my sight; and Israel will become a proverb and a byword among people."

How much more could the Lord God do for Solomon? He gave his servant abundant graces, knowledge, understanding, wisdom, riches and power. Besides that he warned him what would happen and this actually happened and is still happening today.

"This house will become a heap of ruins; everyone passing by it will be astonished and will ask, 'Why has the Lord done thus to this land and to his house?' and they will say, 'Because they foresook the Lord their God and worshipped other gods.'"

There is no doubt Solomon on that day had the most sincere intentions to serve the Lord in an upright way, while the future proved to be very different. He was a man with the mind of wisdom as no other man ever born, and he was at the peak of his and Israel's glory. From his father David he inherited poetical talent and wrote thousands of lyrics, numerous proverbs, wise sayings and epigrams. While David's songs and poems reflected his mystical character, Solomon's were more concerned with human nature, social affairs, justice and injustice, goodness, wickedness, envy, virtue and reward. Although many of the proverbs that were accredited to Solomon were actually collected from folklore, there are still many that are his own:

"The fear of the Lord is the beginning of knowledge; fools despise wisdom and instruction.

Do not plan evil against your neighbor who dwells trustingly beside you.

Do not envy a man of violence and do not choose any of his ways.

A foolish woman is noisy; she is wanton and knows no shame.

Do not reprove a scoffer, or he will hate you; reprove a wise man and he will love you.

Wisdom builds her house, but folly with her own hands tears it down.

A soft answer turns away wrath, but a harsh word stirs up anger.

It is the glory of God to conceal things, but the glory of kings is to search things out.

After finishing the Temple of God Solomon started on a complex of royal buildings surrounding the Temple: his own palace, his government quarters and a separate palace for his Egyptian wife. Rare trees and a profusion of shrubs and flowers were brought from all over and planted to ornament the whole vicinity. If it required seven years to erect the Temple, it took thirteen years to build the adjoining royal palaces which far exceeded the size, splendor and expense of the Temple. Their cost was so astronomical that Solomon had to cede twenty Galilean cities to Hiram, king of Tyre, to pay his debts.

The magnificence and splendor of the king's palace was unique. Solomon's throne was of ivory, overlaid with the finest gold. It had six steps and at the end of each step stood a lion: six to the right and six to the left. The top of the throne was round and had a large lion on each side. There were two hundred shields of purest gold hung on the walls of the palace.

Solomon did not limit himself only to building palaces, he founded several new cities, beautified and strengthened Jerusalem, so that with few exceptions it surpassed all the cities of that time in beauty and riches.

His reign was extended from the Euphrates River to the borders of Egypt. Being a shrewd businessman he built fortified cities to control the principal trade routes between the Euphrates and Nile. In those cities he exacted tolls from the caravans passing through. In southern Palestine he had copper mines and in partnership with Hiram he built a fleet of ships, operated by skillful Phoenician seamen. Ezion-geber grew rapidly into a new port on the Red Sea bringing Solomon a new fortune from trade with Eastern kings.

35. The Stately Visit of Queen of Sheba

In Southern Arabia on the coast of the Red Sea reigned Queen of Sheba. Her kingdom was rich because of substantial trade with caravan merchants passing through the desert. Perhaps she felt threatened or endangered by Solomon's fleet. Whatever was the reason of her most extraordinary visit to King Solomon's court, it proves to be a fascinating detail of the Old Testament.

Caravans passing through the Land of Sheba told fantastic stories about the splendor, riches and wisdom of King Solomon. For a long time the Queen of Sheba was enticed. Were they exaggerations? She decided to leave the kingdom and to travel some fifteen hundred miles to Jerusalem in order to satisfy her curiosity. The dark Queen of Ethiopia, with brown gazelle-like eyes veiled under long dark eyelashes and a mysterious smile upon her oval-shaped face, uttered to her ladies in a soft voice: "Let's go north and find out how King Solomon's regalia measures up to ours. Let us probe his wisdom with riddles and wits."

A caravan was set like had never been seen before. With lavishness of gifts she wanted to outshine Solomon's riches and to win him over as her ally. Beautiful and clever, she made preparations not only adorning herself with precious stones, tiaras and sheer silks, but also with witty questions and riddles, as was the social custom of those days. There are many legendary stories about their conversations and entertainments, but we will limit ourselves to only the facts that are in the Holy Writ. She wanted to test Solomon's reputed wisdom with hard questions. . . .

> *"She came to Jerusalem with a very great retinue,*
> *with camels bearing spices, and very much gold,*
> *and precious stones."*

Jerusalem was prepared to receive the glamorous queen, giving her a cheering reception. Led by jungle elephants, all kinds of animals, servants of all colors and camels laden with gifts it was the showiest parade Jerusalem had ever seen. After the exchange of gifts and the state reception, the king and queen were alone. Now it was time to test the king's wisdom.

> *"She told him all that was on her mind. And Solo-*
> *mon answered all her questions; there was nothing*
> *hidden from the king which he could not explain to*
> *her."*

When the Queen of Sheba saw all the palaces which Solomon had built, the food on his table, the seating of his officials at the state dinners, countless servants and attendants, fine clothing, artistry of ivory, gold, and precious wood, his cupbearers and his burnt offerings which he offered at the Temple, there was no more spirit in her."

> *"And she said to the king, 'The report was true*
> *which I heard in my own land of your affairs and*
> *of your wisdom, but I did not believe the reports*
> *until I came and my own eyes had seen it."*

The king's wisdom and prosperity surpassed all her expectations and the Queen of Sheba admitted in a sincere manner: "Blessed are your servants who stand before you and hear your wisdom. Blessed be the Lord your God, who has delighted in you and set you on the throne of Israel!"

> *"Then she gave the king a hundred and twenty tal-*
> *ents of gold, and a very great quantity of spices*

and precious stones; never again came such an
abundance of spices as these which the Queen of
Sheba gave to King Solomon."

Before leaving for her own country King Solomon gave her
"all her heart desired," besides the bounty of the king's generosity
in gifts to her. She received a great deal.

The Queen of Sheba's long caravan departed, leaving a cloud
of dust behind it. Solomon, although enriched by her visit, felt sad
and lonely in spite of all the wives he had. From the window of
his palace facing south he often looked in the distance with a deep
sigh whispering in the sadness of his mood,

"Vanity, vanity, all is vanity!
The wind blows to the south
and goes round to the north . . .
All streams run to the sea,
but the sea is not full;

The eye is not satisfied with seeing,
nor the ear filled with hearing.

There is nothing new under the sun . . .

I slept but my heart was awake . . .

Many waters cannot quench love,
Neither can floods drown it."

He made sacrifices of burnt offerings just as before, three
times a year. He went to the Temple to worship the Lord, but all
this was done by rote. From his youth he loved foreign women
and married them. The attachment to these pagan women slowly
changed his heart and distanced him from the Lord, the true God.

"Solomon clung to these (wives) in love. He had
seven hundred wives, princesses, and three hundred
concubines; and his wives turned away his heart."

These foreign wives worshipped pagan idols while Solomon,
the man of peace, looked the other way. He considered himself

broadminded and tolerant. To please his wives he permitted the erection of a house of worship for Modech, the pagan god of gentiles, right next to the Temple of God in Jerusalem. He himself entered the pagan house on the hill and burnt incense on pagan altars and sacrificed to their gods. Solomon wanted peaceful co-existence, and in his lack of moral commitment to Yahweh, his own and his people's morality was shattered under the pretense of "toleration."

In the Lord's sight it was a great sin. For the third time the Lord God spoke with reproach to Solomon, the wisest man who ever lived on earth:

> *"Since this has been your mind and you have not kept my covenant and my statutes which I have commanded you, I will surely tear the kingdom from you and will give it to your servant. Yet for the sake of David your father, I will not do it in your days, but I will tear it out of the hand of your son. I will give one tribe to your son for the sake of David and for the sake of Jerusalem which I have chosen."*

Would it have been David he would have fallen on his knees and repented, for he knew, "A broken and contrite heart, O God, thou wilt not despise." Solomon lacked the contrite heart of his father. In his old age a secret revolt arose among the discontented people. Israelites were tired of heavy tax burdens, forced labor, oppression and poverty. Besides unsatisfied people among his own, except the tax-exempted tribe of Juda, there were adversaries among his neighbors: Edomite Hadad, Rezon and Jeroban were the leaders who sympathized with the tax-ridden Israelites. The glorious reign of Solomon came to a deplorable ending. Even the Voice of Eden did not change the state of Solomon's mind. Turning to pagan gods his gift of wisdom vanished. Feeble in mind and body the senile king was approaching his end. After his death he was buried in the City of David. His son Rehoboam was proclaimed as new king in 922 B.C.

King Solomon reigned for forty years (that means a long period of time according to Hebrew calculations.) He was a genius king and organizer. He built the Temple and established the ritual of worship. He wrote several books that are called Hebrew wisdom literature, the Books of Proverbs and Ecclesiastes are literary masterpieces. He wrote most beautiful poetry; his is the passionate love poem with the profoundest religious sense, the Canticle of Canticles or the Song of Solomon.

> *"Make haste, my beloved,*
> *and be like gazelle*
> *or a young stag*
> *upon the mountains of spices,"*

ends the Song of Songs by Solomon.

But in Ecclesiastes 1, 16 he gives a testimony that can be applied to any human heart as long as it pulsates in flesh:

> *I said to myself, 'I have acquired great wisdom,*
> *surpassing all who were over Jerusalem before me;*
> *and my mind has had great experience of wisdom*
> *and knowledge. And I applied my mind to know*
> *wisdom and to know madness and folly. I per-*
> *ceived that this also is but a striving after wind.' "*

How closely these words came to the saying of Jesus one thousand years later when he said: "Consider the lilies of the field, how they grow; they toil not, neither do they spin; and yet I say unto you that even Solomon in all his regalia was not arrayed like one of these."

Chapter VI

The Time of Prophets

36. The Divided Kingdom and Its Prophets

Soon after the death of Solomon the kindgdom of Israel was divided. The young king Rehoboam completely lacked the wisdom and diplomacy of Solomon his father. Since Israel was a dual monarchy the young king had to go to the northern part to receive recognition as king by the northern tribes.

People of the northern tribes gathered in the old shrine at Schechem. Masses were crowding on the slopes of the mountain when on its summit arrived King Rehoboam. People were restless. They were tired of high taxes and the tyranny of Solomon. The elders of the northern tribes offered their allegiance to Rehoboam only if he promised to lighten their yoke which Solomon his father had imposed on them. With the Temple built and royal palaces finished, people now expected some relief and improvement of their condition. Rehoboam listened to the elders, to their counsel and to their reasonings, and he told them that he needed three days to consider the matter.

While people lingered around the shrine tired and hungry, Rehoboam consulted with his friends, the playmates of his childhood, young and inexperienced in government just like himself.

The counsel they gave him was just the opposite of the elders. They told him not to give in, to show right from the beginning who was king and ruler. Intoxicated with pride from new power, after the three days of recession, King Rehoboam stood again on top of the hill of Schechem in all his splendor and proclaimed: "My father made your yoke heavy; I will make it heavier. My father used the whip on you, but I will use the lash."

There was a gasp of horror in the shocked crowd. Jeroboam,

a young revolutionary, took lead of the angered and confused people. Someone in the crowd started an old battle song and soon the whole crowd on the mountain side chanted:

> *"What part have we in David?*
> *We have no lot in the son of Jesse.*
> *To your tents, O Israel!*
> *Look now to your own house, David."*

With this song on their lips and new patriotism in their hearts the Israelites departed to their tents. Ten northern tribes anointed Jeroboam as their king and called their kingdom Israel. Besides the tribe of Judah which was always a privileged tribe because David and Solomon both came from Judah, only one other tribe remained loyal to the small southern kingdom. The two tribes established their capital at Jerusalem. From then on their kingdom was called Judah.

As long as Rehoboam lived he was at war with Jeroboam. It took fifty years of civil war until the northern and southern parts accepted themselves as two separate kingdoms.

The moral decline in the northern kingdom was surprisingly fast. Since Jeroboam did not want his people to go to Jerusalem to worship the Lord, he established two old shrines, one in Bethel and another in Dan. There he built a house of worship in each city setting up golden bulls imitating Solomon's Temple, where two animals stood on either side of the Ark. It pleased many, Canaanites especially since the symbol of Baal was a bull, and also Israelites who always had an inclination to idol worship. Soon Israelites and the rest started to worship the golden bulls and forgot about Yahweh, God of Abraham, Isaac and Moses.

From time to time God sent prophets to warn the kings and people, calling them to mend their ways and return to the one true God. So Amos warned Jeroboam and people of Samaria, Osee predicted the Assyrian captivity, and Elijah, the greatest prophet since Moses, with burning zeal called Israelites to stop worshipping Baal and to return to the right ways of the Lord.

37. The Prophet Elijah

Elijah lived in the reign of Ahab and his fanatically pagan wife Jezebel, daughter of the King of Sidon, (circa 923-902 B.C.). At her request Ahab built a temple to the sun god Baal in Samaria. Besides worship of the bull or calf the immoral worship was introduced of Baal and Moloch to whom children and young maidens were sacrificed. Jezebel had four hundred and fifty priests supported by the state who worshipped idols while Ahab put the priests of the Lord to death.

The injustices and grave sins of Ahab and his wife Jezebel were multiplying when one day as though from nowhere suddenly appeared Elijah, clad in rough sheep's skin with a staff in his hand. During that time one of the droughts which periodically afflict the Middle East was in progress. Elijah, associating the drought as a punishment from the Lord for Ahab's sinfulness, brought a warning to the king: "I swear by the life of the Lord the God of Israel whose servant I am," cried the prophet, "that there shall be neither dew nor rain these coming years unless I give the word."

He left Ahab as suddenly as he arrived leaving him angry and perplexed. Ahab sent his spies to look for Elijah so that he could put him away, but for three years they could not find even a trace of him. There was not a drop of rain all this time in Israel and the earth was parched and cattle were dying from thirst. Then Ahab received a message that Elijah was back in town. The king went out to meet him.

"As soon as Ahab saw Elijah, he said to him, 'Is it you, you who trouble of Israel?' 'It is not I who trouble Israel,' he replied, 'but you and your father's family, by forsaking the commandments of the Lord and following Baal. But now, send and summon all Israel to meet me on Mount Carmel, and the four hundred and fifty prophets of Baal with them and the goddess Asherah, who is Jezebel's pensioner."

There was such authority in the prophet's voice and burning

zeal in his eyes, that even king Ahab did not dare to contradict. By some unexplained compulsion he had to obey the orders of the one who spoke for the Lord, who said, "Whose servant I am," and who called himself a prophet of Yahweh. In our days we often use the word "prophet" to describe one who predicts the future. To the Israelites a prophet was God's spokesman, one who spoke for God now in the present with any prediction of future being only incidental.

At Ahab's order Israelites and the prophets of Baal assembled on Mt. Carmel.

"How long will you sit on the fence?" thundered Elijah's voice addressing the assembly. "If the Lord is God, follow him; but if Baal, then follow him."

With so much power had no one yet spoken to them. This voice made people shiver with fear and they were dumbfounded. They knew there were only two alternatives for them: either to accept God or to reject him, nothing in-between.

Seeing the effect of his words on the people, Elijah challenged the prophets of Baal: 'I am the only prophet of the Lord still left, but there are four hundred and fifty prophets of Baal. Bring two bulls for offering. You shall invoke your god by name and I will invoke the Lord by name, and the god who answers by fire, he is God."

With a feeling of relief the mass of assembled people shouted their approval. They liked the proposal of supernatural intervention.

The priests of Baal, clad in their purple ceremonial garments and crowned with laurel, slew an ox. They erected an altar, put the killed ox on it and dancing around it crying, "Baal hear us!" They called from morning until noon, but no fire came from heaven. Then Elijah mocking them, shouted, "Cry louder, perhaps your god is on a journey or asleep and you have to awaken him." The prophets of Baal cried louder and louder until the evening came, but there was no answer to their cries.

Then Elijah told the people to come on his side where he had erected an altar using twelve stone, one for each tribe of Israel.

Fire fell from the sky and the whole offering was consumed.

He placed wood on it and killed a bull. Then he poured water upon the victim until it ran down on every side filling the trench
around the altar. Raising his hands toward heaven Elijah cried in
a loud voice, "Lord God, let it be known today that thou art God
in Israel and that I am thy servant who does your will. Answer
me, O Lord, answer me, that this people may know that thou, O
Lord, art God, and that thou hast turned their hearts back."

Fire fell from the sky and the whole offering was consumed
by it instantly. People seeing it fell on their faces and called: "The
Lord, he is God; the Lord, he is God!"

Being in full control of the people Elijah cried, Seize the
prophets of Baal, let not one of them escape."

The crowd brought the prophets of Baal to the Valley of
Kidron and killed them all there.

Elijah prostrated himself on top of Mount Carmel in praise
and thanksgiving. Then he prayed to the Lord to refresh the earth
with water. And behold, a little cloud no bigger than the palm of
a hand arose from the Mediterranean Sea, near the horizon. It
spread itself over the skies of Israel and a thirst-quenching rain
fell in abundance.

Three years passed and Ahab died from the spear of a Syrian
on the battlefield. Some time after, the wickedly evil queen Jezebel
was cast down from the window of her palace, as the new king
Jehu was passing through the town. She was trampled over by
royal chariots and the dogs came and ate her flesh, just as Elijah
once predicted.

Elijah remained a true prophet of the Lord who never spoke
to please kings or people, nor for his own safety, but proclaimed
the will of God.

As his successor, he trained Elisha.

"The spirit of Elijah rests in Elisha," said those who knew
them both. Many miracles happened during Elijah's life, like his
calling down fire from heaven, and the angel that ministered to
him when he was a weary sleeper, and his most legendary ride to
heaven in the golden chariot. To get closer acquainted with his
extraordinary life one has to turn to the Holy Scripture.

38. Jonah — a Prophet for Gentiles

Through many centuries God proved again and again a steadfast love for his chosen people. Although mankind gradually rose to a knowledge of God, it was different with Adam. Adam had a complete knowledge of God from the moment he was created. He could see God, able to converse with his Creator as soon as his eyes were open for the first time. Things changed after the fall —the more men sinned the further away they distanced themselves from the Lord.

To preserve Israel from idolatry and to keep the Messianic hope alive, God sent one prophet after another. Their purpose was to keep Israel aware of their great destiny. Besides that each prophet taught a lesson, or rather God taught through the prophets, the relation between Creator and the men who were chosen people. Moses proclaimed the God of justice, the Lord who punishes and rewards. The relationship between Abraham and God was one of deep trust — faithfulness. But between David and the Lord it was a relationship between son and Father. In years to come, through the prophet Osee God taught a new lesson: the love of God was symbolized in the love of husband and wife. The prophet Osee was the first one to emphasize God's love for Israel, and later Christ's love for the Church, as a relationship between husband and wife. John the Baptist called our Lord the "Bridegroom" and also Jesus described himself so.

An entirely new lesson in the love of God was taught through the prophet Jonah. For those days and beliefs it was quite a revolutionary thought. Jonah was called to prophesy right after Eliseus. Until then Israelites thought that the Lord God was the God of Israel who had nothing to do with heathens, at least that he was not personally interested in their well-being.

In those days Israelites lived in prosperity and bounty. The daughters of Sion adorned themselves in fine clothes and wore tinkling bracelets around their arms and ankles. Their homes were decorated with ivory and gold; one rich feast was surpassed by another even more gay and immoral than the ones preceding.

Jonah, son of Amittai, "the truthful one," heard the Voice of Eden one day. The Lord was sending Jonah on a special mission to Nineveh, the heathen capital of Assyria, to call the pagan Assyrians to repentance.

"Arise," said the Lord to Jonah. "Go to Nineveh and preach there, for their wickedness has come up before me."

How could Jonah believe his own ears? Nineveh—the grandest city with a wall so wide around it that on its top three chariots could race side by side! With its 120,000 inhabitants worshipping idols and practicing wickedness, how could Jonah teach them about the true God? And why? What if they repented and God showed them mercy? Jonah knew too well how merciful was the Lord to all those who repent. Weren't they the most threatening enemies of Israelites who are always ready to devour them? Why spare them? Let them be destroyed, after all they deserve it! How could he be a prophet to those idolaters? And what would his own people say if he went to Nineveh to save them? In the eyes of the Israelites he would be a false prophet; maybe they would even stone him.

Terrified, Jonah boarded a Phoenician ship at Joppa, to run away from the face of the Lord, heading for Tharsis in Spain. As soon as the ship left the harbor a great storm arose. The sea swelled and heaved tossing the ship, threatening to sink it. Frightened sailors threw all cargo on board into the sea in order to lighten the vessel. While the sea still roared and billowed each of them started to pray to his own god. Jonah was below in the bottom of the ship fast asleep. The sailors decided there must be someone on the ship who had a guilty conscience, and they proposed to cast lots so they might know why this evil had come upon them. Jonah was awakened to cast his lot—and the lot fell upon him. He confessed his sins saying, "Take me up and cast me into the sea, and sea shall be calm to you."

The sailors, unwilling to throw Jonah overboard, rowed with all their might to reach shore, where they wanted to set him out in safety. But the sea swelled ever higher. They had to toss praying

While praying Jonah tossed and wallowed around in the whale's stomach until the fish vomited him upon the shore.

Jonah over the rail. Once in the water Jonah was immediately swallowed by an approaching whale, and the sea calmed down.

Jonah, fully alive in the roomy belly of the great creature of the ocean, was contrite. He begged for the mercy of the Lord and kept on praying.

"I am cast away, out of the sight of thy eyes; but yet I shall see thy holy temple again," whispered Jonah in the darkness. While praying he tossed and wallowed around the whale's stomach until he made the huge fish nauseated. After three days it vomited him upon the shore.

Before Jonah could understand what had happened, he heard the Voice of the Lord a second time.

"Arise, go into Nineveh."

Jonah knew the Lord really meant it. There was just one way to go now—the way of obedience. He rose up and without delay went in the direction of the doomed city. Once inside the wall of Nineveh he walked through the streets, calling out: "Yet forty days and Nineveh shall be destroyed!"

People gathered on the street corners, in the squares and market places to listen to the strange prophet. They took his message seriously and were frightened by it. The king heard the voice of Jonah and heeded the prophet's call. He put on a sackcloth and sat in ashes. He ordered all his people, from the greatest to the least, to fast and do penance in order to appease the anger of God. And in pagan Nineveh there happened what did not happen in chosen cities. . . .

Meanwhile Jonah went some distance out of the city to see what would happen. With prejudice in his heart, ingrained through many generations, he could not understand why the Lord Almighty should be concerned about these idol worshippers, while at the same time the Israelites were bowing more and more to the calves of gold and other idols, turning away from the one true God. Why did not the God of Abraham, Moses and Isaac send a mighty prophet to them?

Forty days passed, and Jonah saw that Nineveh was spared. He was angry. Troubled that he would be considered a false prophet by his own people he was afraid to go back to Israel. He wanted to die right there. God, however, showed his prophet how unreasonable his anger was. When Jonah was asleep during the night a large vine grew near him and shadowed him from the scorching rays of the sun. But on the following morning God caused a worm to eat away the roots of the plant, and it withered just as fast as it had popped out. When the sun and hot desert wind was again broiling Jonah's head, he scolded the withered plant for not giving him shade. His anger about the injustice of the Lord was so great that he stretched himself out on the ground and decided not to move until he died. God, always patient and understanding, taught Jonah a lesson:

"You are grieved for the ivy for which you did not labor, neither made it grow; which came up in the night and perished in the night; and should I not spare Nineveh, the great city?"

Jonah realized that Yahweh was not merely God of Israel, but the one true God of all mankind, including heathens. The Messiah himself would speak of Jonah condemning the hard-hearted people: "The men of Nineveh shall rise in judgment with this generation and shall condemn it, because they did penance at the preaching of Jonah." And "A sign shall not be given it but the sign of Jonah the prophet."

39. The End of the Northern and Southern Kingdoms

The northern kingdom of Israel having once started to worship Baal, degenerated rapidly. Without God's help they were weak and the Assyrians made them their vassals. Salmanassar, the king of Assyria, requested high taxes from Samaria. When they refused to pay the tribute Salmanassar conquered the country and carried the ten tribes of Israel into captivity in 722 B.C. In exile the tribes intermingled with Assyrians, but there is very little said about them in the Bible. The poorer people stayed in the country, but they also mixed with Arabs, Cuthites and others. They called themselves Samaritans. Their country got the name Palestine which it was known as at the time of Christ. To a certain degree they followed Moses' teachings, developing their own scriptures.

The southern kingdom of Judah consisted of the large tribe of Judah and the smaller tribe of Benjamin. According to God's promise to David, their ways were less idolatrous than the kings of the north. Their rule was longer, but because of their prosperity they were a constant prey to their larger neighbors. Also, the measure of sins of Judah was filling up their cup, and God delivered them into captivity in Babylon in 605 B.C. The second deportation occurred in 597 B.C. Finally Nebuchodonosor, infuriated by the Jews who did not subject themselves to his rule, destroyed the temple of Solomon and completely ruined Jerusalem in 586 B.C.

"Oh, all you that pass by the way, attend and see if there be any sorrow like unto my sorrow," lamented Jeremiah about the beloved city.

40. The Prophet Isaiah

While Osee and Amos were preaching in the northern kingdom a great prophet arose in Judah at the same time. Sirach called Isaiah the great prophet, "With a great Spirit he saw the things that are to come to pass at last. . . . He showed what should come to pass for ever, and secret things before they came."

Isaiah more than any prophet, with the clear vision of the Messiah, preached the kingdom of God. Born and raised in Jerusalem Isaiah, the son of Amos, was a nobleman, highly educated and wealthy. Just as any other of his class he enjoyed a happy period of peace and prosperity in the mid-eighth century B.C. His calling to serve the Lord came suddenly and unexpectedly while he was worshipping God in the House of the Lord, the great Jerusalem Temple. At that time King Uzziah was dying from leprosy, and spiritual leprosy was seizing the Judeans who turned away from the Lord and brought idols into their homes and temples to worship.

While offering his sacrifice in the inner sanctuary, Isaiah suddenly found himself in a state of rapture. Everything vanished. He —all alone—stood on the planet earth while the heavens opened and he looked at the Lord God's blinding glory.

> *The Lord seated on a throne high and exalted and the skirt of his robe filled the Temple. About him were attendant seraphim, and each had six wings; one pair covered his face and one pair his feet, and one pair spread in flight. They were calling ceaselessly to one another,*
>
> *"Holy, holy, holy is the Lord of Hosts: the whole earth is full of his glory."*

The whole Temple was trembling from their powerful voices. Isaiah trembled from fear. Then he heard the Voice from heaven, "Whom shall I send, and who will go for us?

In his youthful eagerness and in the ecstacy of his spirit Isaiah cried, "Behold, me! Send me!"

But at this moment he became aware of his sinfulness and how unworthy he stood in the presence of the Lord.

"Woe is me! I am lost, for I am a man of unclean lips and I dwell among a people of unclean lips; yet with these eyes I have seen the King, the Lord of Hosts."

Isaiah's repentance was deep and sincere. One of the seraphim came down with a glowing coal which he took from the altar with a pair of tongs, and touched Isaiah's lips.

"See, this touched your lips," spoke the heavenly being, "Your iniquity is removed and your sin is wiped away."

"Whom shall I send? Who will go for us?" the Lord asked again.

"Here am I; send me," answered Isaiah.

"Go and tell this people," was the message from heaven. "You may listen and listen, but you will not understand. You may look and look again, but you will never know. This people's wits are dulled, their ears are deafened and their eyes are blinded."

Isaiah understood his order: he had to preach to his people without having any illusion that they would accept it or that it would change them in the least way. He had to do it because it was the right thing to do, disregarding how hopeless his task seemed. Troubled by this thought, he asked, "How long, O Lord?"

"Until cities fall in ruins and are deserted," came the answer from the throne. "Until the Lord has sent all mankind far away, and the whole country is one vast desolation. Even if a tenth part of its people remain there, they too will be exterminated."

Young and determined Isaiah set on his way to preach the doom of his nation. Being well versed in language he spoke in a sublime, eloquent manner to the crowds on the street corners who listened to him and who, smiling or sneering, returned to their flesh pots and joys of high living. "There were prophets of doom before him," they thought, "and only simpletons would take them seriously." Such was the opinion of the majority of Jerusalemites. But Isaiah continued to warn and defy one king after another, telling them about fearful calamities that were to befall their country unless they did penance.

"Hear the word of the Lord," he called. "Wash yourselves, be clean. Take away the evil of your devices from my eyes; cease to do perversely; learn to do well; seek judgment. If your sins be as scarlet they shall be as white as snow: if they will be red as a crimson, they shall be as white as wool."

People did not heed the warnings. They lived in comfort wondering why they should worry about the future when today was good and bright. But the threatening powers were already gathering around Judea. By the time Ahaz ascended to Judah's throne Assyria was looking at it as an eagle on its prey. Judea was a fertile crescent waiting to be swallowed with all its trimmings. Since King Ahaz refused the alliance between Syria and Israel Assyrians invaded Judea in 733 B.C. The king and people "were shaken like forest trees in the wind." The only choice Ahaz saw now was to become the vassal of Assyria. At this critical moment

Isaiah went to the king and urged him not to make an alliance with Assyria but to trust in God alone. Ahaz did not believe that God would save them from disaster, although Isaiah offered a sign from God.

"I will not put the Lord to the test by asking for a sign," Ahaz cried with scorn.

Disregarding the king's protest, Isaiah, provoked to anger, gave a sign:

> *"Must you also wear out the patience of my God?*
> *Therefore the Lord himself will give you a sign:*
> *A virgin shall conceive and bear a Son, and shall*
> *call his name Immanuel."*

With this prophecy Isaiah foresaw the birth of Christ seven centuries ahead.

Ahaz disregarded Isaiah's advice and entered into agreement with Assyria. A great price was paid for this alliance: all treasures from the Jerusalem Temple were removed and transferred to Assyria, Judea became a vassal to Assyria and the newly erected altars in the Jerusalem Temple were rededicated to Assyrian deities.

Broken-hearted and distressed, Isaiah withdrew from public life into one of the caves to lead a life of prayer and penance. In 715 B.C. King Ahaz died. Heir to the throne was Hezekiah, a determined man faithful to the one true God. His first deed was removing the Assyrian altars from the Temple. Next he built a new water tunnel, since the Assyrians in order to harass people, cut off the water supply from Jerusalem. The tunnel was 1777 feet — 553.94 meters—long, cut through solid rock to supply water for Jerusalem.

Then he sent for Isaiah to ask the prophet's advice on whether or not to join with others in revolt against Assyria. Isaiah told him the same thing he told Ahaz:

> *"Do not become part of the conspiracy. He shall not*
> *come into the city, not shoot an arrow there, nor*

come before it with the shield, for I will defend this
city, to save it, for mine own sake, and for my ser-
vant David's sake."

It was an astounding declaration with the enemy surrounding the city. But during the night a miracle happened. An angel of the Lord passed through the camp of the sleeping Assyrian troops and struck them with an unknown malady that in one night ended the lives of 185,000 men. Those who were left alive retreated in a great hurry.

The people of Jerusalem rejoiced. They sang praises to Yahweh, who alone was their God. But how long was this to last? Soon they forgot it and put all their trust in political maneuverings rather than in the Lord.

The warnings from Isaiah were sounded again on the corners of the streets and in the marketplaces of Jerusalem. Through Isaiah the voice of the Lord spoke: "Ah, Assyria, the rod of my anger, the staff of my fury!"

Isaiah knew that destruction of Jerusalem was only a matter of a short time. Because of his predictions he was quite unpopular among his people, even despised.

"Behold, the days come, that all that is in your house
shall be carried into Babylon: nothing shall be left,
says the Lord. And your sons they shall be eunuchs
in the palace of the king of Babylon."

King Hezekiah did not want to hear such prophecy and was content with "peace in our time." When he died his son Manasseh was proclaimed king. As a boy he was already mean, with an inclination to evil and as king he became a tyrant. He persecuted the priests and the prophets, shedding innocent blood until no one in Jerusalem was safe. His reign, vicious and wicked, was a long one, from the age of twelve until he was sixty-four. It is told that Isaiah was put to death by this cruel king, tied to a log and sawed in two.

It was Isaiah to whom the Messianic hope was revealed. His

prophecies are so clear and detailed that one would suppose Isaiah had lived at the same time as Christ and not seven hundred years before. Some of his prophecies are used in our liturgical texts even today, never losing the freshness of originality:

> *"A child is born to us, a son is given; and the government will be upon his shoulder, and his name will be called "Wonderful, Counselor, Mighty God, Everlasting Father, Prince of Peace.' "*

> *"God himself will come and save you; then shall eyes of the blind be opened and the ears of the deaf be unstopped."*

He also foresaw the passion of our Lord when he prophesied:

> *"There is no beauty in him, nor comeliness. Despised, and the most abject of men, a man of sorrows. He has borne our infirmities; he was wounded for our iniquities; he was bruised for our sins; and by his bruises we are healed. The Lord has laid on him the iniquity of us all. He was offered because it was his own will, and he opened not his mouth. He shall be led as a sheep to the slaughter or a sheep before the shearers, oppressed and condemned, he was taken away, and who would have thought any more of his destiny?*

But in all this sadness and iniquity Isaiah saw a new day dawning, a day of hope and salvation.

> *"The Gentiles shall beseech him and his sepulchre shall be glorious."*

As John the Apostle saw the new Jerusalem rising at the end of time, so Isaiah predicted the second coming of Christ:

> *"For behold, the Lord will come in fire,*
> *and his chariots like a stormwind,*
> *to render his anger in fury,*

and his rebuke with flames of fire.
For by fire will the Lord execute judgment,
and by his sword, upon all flesh;
and those slain by the Lord shall be many.

"For the new heavens and the new earth
which I will make
shall remain before me, says the Lord."

41. The Babylonian Captivity

Many prophets were sent to the chosen people to lead them back to righteous ways. After Isaiah another prophet—Jeremiah—was warning people, but their ears remained deaf. They gave themselves to the vile practices of idolatry, and persecuting and even executing many of the prophets of God. In vain Jeremiah called them to repentance. They went so far as to make sacrifices of their own children to the pagan god Moloch. The Lord lost his patience and delivered them into the hands of their enemy.

In 587 B.C. during the reign of Ezekiel, Nebuchodonosor crushed the Judean revolt and destroyed Jerusalem. The whole city became flames and ruins. The Jerusalem Temple was consumed by fire and the sacred vessels were carried off. All the people who escaped the sword were led into captivity in Babylon, leaving behind the once splendid city of Jerusalem — now only a heap of ruins. According to God's promise Jeremiah remained in Jerusalem.

"For I will surely save you, and you shall not fall by the sword, because you have put trust in me," said the Lord to Jeremiah.

Sitting on the ruins of the desolate city the old prophet cried and lamented the destruction of Jerusalem and the fate of his people:

How lonely sits the city that was full of people!
How like a widow has she become, she that was
great among nations!

She that was a princess among the cities
has become a vassal.
She weeps bitterly in the night,
tears on her cheeks;
among all her lovers
she has none to comfort her;
all her friends have dealt
treacherously with her,
they have become her enemies.

Judah has gone into exile
because of affliction
and hard servitude;
she dwells now among the nations,
but finds no resting place;
her pursuers have all overtaken her
in the midst of her distress.

Jerusalem sinned grievously,
therefore she became filthy;
all who honored her despise her,
for they have seen her nakedness;
yea, she herself groans,
and turns her face away.

For these things I weep;
my eyes flow with tears;
for a comforter is far from me,
one to revive my courage;
my children are desolate,
for the enemy has prevailed.

The Lord has done what he purposed,
has carried out his threat;
as he ordained long ago,
he has demolished without pity,
he has made the enemy rejoice over you,
and exalted the might of your foes.

Cry aloud to the Lord!
O Daughter of Zion.
Let tears stream down like a torrent
day and night!
Give yourself no rest,
your eyes no respite!

Remember, O Lord, what has befallen us;
behold, and see our disgrace!
Our inheritance has been turned
over to strangers,
our homes to aliens.
We have become orphans, fatherless;
our mothers are like widows.

But thou, O Lord, dost reign for ever;
Thy throne endures to all generations.
Why dost thou so long forsake us?
Restore us to thyself, O Lord,
that we may be restored!
Renew our days of old!
O hast thou utterly rejected us?
Are thou exceedingly angry with us?

Jeremiah, however, was not without consolation. He knew that Israel would be restored and that God would make a new covenant with his people.

"The days shall come," says the Lord, "and I will make a new covenant with the house of Israel and with the house of Juda. Not according to the covenants which I made with their fathers, which they made void. I will give my law and will write it on their hearts, and I will be their God and they shall by my people. I will forgive their iniquity and I will remember their sin no more."

Looking at the ruins of their sacred and beloved Jerusalem, the remaining Jews cried day and night, "What shall we do?"

Jeremiah told them to stay where they were. But this kind of advice was against their thinking. They wanted to be safe, secure . . . and the remaining Jews set out on the road to Egyypt, seeking refuge in the land which their forefathers left. They took Jeremiah with them. As in Jerusalem, Jeremiah preached disaster to those in the land of the Nile. He prophesied that Assyrians would conquer Egypt the same way they conquered Judea. Seeing that the Hebrews turned to Egyptian idols, he warned them to their great displeasure.

> *"Therefore hear ye the word of the Lord, all Judah that dwell in the land of Egypt. . . . Behold, I will watch over them for evil, and not for good: and all the men of Judah that are in the land of Egypt shall be consumed by the sword and by famine, until there be an end of them."*

For this Jeremiah was stoned by his own people, and he died in Egypt.

Those who were in Babylonian captivity had better fortune. Babylon in those days was a beautiful city, built with strength and splendor. Babylonians treated exiles with kindness. Hebrews were allowed to practice their religion, assemble freely and speak their own language. They soon adjusted to the new life and situated themselves comfortably. Although life for them was even prosperous, the only thing they longed for and wanted was to get back to their own land to rebuild their sacred city, Jerusalem.

"How long, O Lord, how long?" groaned the captive people.

But the Lord God did not abandon his people, even during their captivity. He sent the prophet Ezekiel to instruct them. After Ezekiel there was Daniel who charmed the Babylonian king with his wisdom and the gift of prophecy to interpret dreams.

For one hundred and fifty years Israel—the northern kingdom —was in captivity, and the Judeans for seventy years, as Jeremiah had foretold. Daniel predicted that from the day on which the order should be given to rebuild Jerusalem until the death of the Messiah, there would remain only seventy weeks of years, that is

490 years. In this way Hebrews knew not only the family from which the Savior would come, the root of Jesse, from the house of David—but also the city in whch he would be born, as prophet Micheas told in Babylon:

> *"And thou, Bethlehem Ephrata, art a little one among the thousands of Judah; out of thee shall he come forth unto me that is to be the ruler of Israel; and his going forth is from the beginning, from the days of eternity."*

Sufferings of the captivity in Babylon had brought the Jewish people to a sense of their duty. There they were more closely united than in their own land, and they worshipped God with greater fervor and sincerity.

42. The Son of Man

During the Babylonian captivity there were two prophets who strengthened the spirit of the exiles. One was Ezekiel and another Daniel. Both started their mission as very young men, in their early twenties. Both had prophetic visions and revelations not only about the coming Messiah but also about the end of mankind, the last judgment and the everlasting rule of the Son of Man.

Ezekiel was a member of a distinguished priestly family. Life for Ezekiel, as most of the Jews (the word comes from "Judeans") in Babylon, was comfortable. He started his public service of priesthood when he was thirty. Soon after he had a vision. Ezekiel tells about his vision:

> *"In the thirtieth year, in the fourth month, on the fifth day of the month, as I was among the exiles by the river Chebar, the heavens were opened, and I saw visions of God. . . .*
>
> *As I looked, behold, a stormy wind came out of the north, and a great cloud, with brightness round about it, and fire flashing forth continually, and in*

*the midst of the fire, as it were gleaming bronze.
And from the midst of it came the likeness of four
living creatures. . . . And each went straight forward; wherever the spirit would go. . . . In the midst
of the living creatures there was something that
looked like burning coals of fire, like torches moving to and fro among the living creatures; . . .*

*Over the head of the living creatures there was
the likeness of a firmament, shining like crystal,
spread out above the heads. . . . And above the
firmament over their heads there was the likeness
of a throne, in appearance like sapphire; and
seated above was a likeness as it were of a human
form. . . . .*

*Such was the appearance of the likeness of the
glory of the Lord. And when I saw it, I fell upon
my face, and I heard the voice of one speaking:
"Son of man, stand upon your feet, and I will
speak with you."*

The creatures Ezekiel saw in this vision had the form of men
with four faces and each had wings. Their legs sparkled like
bronze. Their wings touched one another as they went straight
forward. Each had the face of a man, face of a lion, an ox, and of
an eagle at the back. Christianity describes these symbols as the
four evangelists Matthew, Mark, Luke and John.

Hearing the voice of the Lord, strength returned to Ezekiel.
For seven days after that vision Ezekiel was in a trance until he
heard the Voice of God again.

Son of man,* I make you a watchman in the house of the
Lord."

Several revelations were made manifest to Ezekiel. These he
had to teach to his countrymen. Until now they believed that sin
was a communal thing — everyone suffers because of one who
trespasses the law of God. There was a popular proverb among

---

*Here the term "Son of Man" is used for the first time in the Bible.

the chosen people: "The fathers have eaten sour grapes and the children's teeth are set on edge."

Not so, explained the Lord to Ezekiel. Sin is individual. Therefore repentance and salvation must be individual. For more than twenty years Ezekiel, preaching to his captive brethren, kept alive in them the flame of longing for their Mother Jerusalem, always sighing in his prayers, "O Lord, how long?"

He was preaching a new lesson, an entirely new outlook which was not known before:

> *Israel says, "The way of the Lord is not just." O house of Israel, are my ways not just? Is it not your ways that are not just? Therefore I will judge you, everyone according to his ways, says the Lord God. Repent and turn from all your transgressions, lest iniquity be your ruin. Cast away from you all your transgressions which you have committed against me, and get yourselves a new heart and a new spirit! For I have no pleasure in the death of anyone, so turn, and live."*

There was another important revelation which God disclosed through Ezekiel: the idea of the Good Shepherd. Probably David already had that idea when he sang "The Lord is my Shepherd," but it was not a common concept to the Israelites. In a vision the Lord God taught Ezekiel to preach that Yahweh would be the earthly Shepherd, a descendant of David, who would not be a mighty king on earth, but who would be God's servant prince, a faithful one.

> *For thus says the Lord, "I myself will search for my sheep and I will seek them out. As a shepherd seeks out his flock. . . . And I, the Lord, will be their God, and my servant David shall be prince among them."*

This prophecy was taken literally by exiles, thinking that the Messiah would come and lead them out of bondage back to Jerusalem where they would sit again next to full fleshpots and gaze in the green pastures. This prophecy came true in the time of the Messiah, when the Jews were gathered in their own land and the Temple of Jerusalem was rebuilt again.

Even though there was no Temple, the exiles in Babylon learned another lesson from Ezekiel: that God may be worshipped anywhere. They gathered in small groups for instruction and worship. They called the places of gathering synagogues. Since Israel was not a political nation anymore, it discovered itself to be a spiritual community, keeping faithfully the holiness of the Sabbath, the ancient festivals and their peculiar diet. The Lord had revealed to Ezekiel:

> *"Fear not, for I have redeemed you; I have called*
> *you by your name; you are mine. . . . I am the*
> *First and the Last; and beside me there is no God."*

43. Daniel's Vision of the Last Judgement

Daniel as a young lad, with three other Hebrew boys, was selected to be trained for the king of Babylon's service. They were given rich food and wine just as other courtiers. Daniel and his friends refused to take that food and instead asked to be fed only vegetables. After three years of being faithful to Jewish dietary laws the boys were found in superior health and wisdom to all the others.

At that time Nebuchodonosor, king of Babylon, was so very greatly troubled by his dreams that no one could explain. Worst of all, he could not remember his dream, that repeatedly troubled him. Daniel was called in and he explained what the dream meant:

> *O king, your thoughts came into your mind upon*
> *your bed, what should come to pass hereafter. And*
> *you saw a great image whose form was terrible. Its*
> *head was of fine gold, its breast and arms of silver,*

the belly and thighs of brass, legs of iron, and feet part iron, part clay. And there was a stone cut out without the labor of hands, and it smote first the feet and broke them to pieces, and it became like chaff of the summer threshing floors. And the wind carried them away. The stone that smote the image became a great mountain and filled the whole earth."

That was the dream! King Nebuchodonosor felt relieved from the unknown terror. "Of truth it is that your God is the God of gods and the revealer of secrets!" exclaimed the heathen king.

Daniel was showered with gifts. But the pagan astrologers who could not interpret the dream and all the magicians fell into the king's disgrace. Recognition of the "God of Daniel" did not mean the conversion of the king's heart. Soon after that he made a golden statue of himself, ninety feet tall and commanded all his subjects to be present at the dedication. When the flutes, harps and other instruments started to play, everyone had to fall down to worship the statue. All did except three of Daniel's friends. Infuriated over their disobedience, the king ordered them to be cast into the glowing fire of the furnace. Everyone was watching. To everybody's surprise the three young men did not burn, but walked in the midst of the flaming furnace like in a promenade in a park on a sunny day, singing hymns of praise to the Lord. "And the Lord himself was in their midst."

"Did we not cast three men bound into the fire?" called Nebuchodonosor.

"True, O king," answered the officer of the guard.

"Look, I see four men loose, walking in the midst of the fire, and they have no hurt. And the fourth is the Son of God!" shouted the astonished king.

The boys were released and the king made a decree that every people, nation and language, who speaks anything amiss against their God shall be cut to pieces, "Because there is no other God that can deliver in this manner."

So the exiles became the living witnesses of one God to the pagan gentiles and the true idea of God started to spread beyond the Jewish community. King Nebuchodonosor, after severe trials, recognized the one true God. He made to all his subjects a surprising revelation:

> *"At the end of the days I, Nebuchodonosor, lifted*
> *my eyes to heaven, and my reason returned to me,*
> *and I blessed the Most High, and praised and*
> *honored him who lives for ever;*
>
>> *for his dominion is everlasting dominion,*
>> *and his kingdom endures from generation*
>> *to generation. . . .*
>
> *All his works are right and his ways are just; and*
> *those who walk in pride he is able to abase."*

These were the last words of the king of Babylon, the first pagan king converted to the one true God. Daniel also converted King Darius the Mede, who conquered Babylon after the death of Nebuchodonosor.

Before the end of his life Daniel saw apocalyptic dreams— visions, which were closely related to St. John's visions described in the Book of Revelation.

The first vision was about the four winds stirring up the great sea—a lion with eagle wings, a bear with three ribs in its mouth, a leopard with wings of a bird on its back and four heads. The fourth beast was most terrible and strong, with iron teeth to devour and with ten horns on its head.

The next vision of Daniel revealed:

> *"As I looked, thrones were placed*
>> *and one that was ancient of days*
>> *took his seat;*
> *his raiment was white as snow,*
> *and the hair of his head like pure wool;*
> *his throne was fiery flames,*
>> *its wheels were burning fire.*

A stream of fire issued and came forth
from before him;
and ten thousand times ten
thousand stood before him;
the court sat in judgment,
and the books were opened."

These visions were explained to Daniel by the Angel Gabriel who stood near by. "The Ancient in Days" is God who reigns over all ages. In these visions Daniel gives a clear idea of the Messiah and of the kingdom of God. Some historians do not agree as to what time exactly the book of Daniel was written. However, no matter how late it was written, it was known before the coming of Christ.

The last vision Daniel related was about "after-life" which affirms God's steadfast love and his infinite justice.

". . . and behold, with the clouds of heaven
there came one like the son of man,
and he came to the Ancient of Days
and was presented before him.
And to him was given dominion
and glory and kingdom,
that all people, nations, and languages
should serve him;
His dominion is an everlasting dominion,
which shall not pass away,
and his kingdom one
that shall not be destroyed."

"At that time shall arise Michael,
the great prince who has charge of your people.
And there shall be a time of trouble, such as
never has been since there was a nation till that time;
but at that time your people shall be delivered, every
one whose name shall be found written in the book.
And many of those who sleep in the dust of the earth

shall awake, some to everlasting life, and some to
shame and everlasting contempt, and those who are wise
shall shine like the brightness of the firmament; and those
who turn many to righteousness, like the stars
for ever and ever."

Through his visions Daniel grasped the concept of hell and of everlasting life in union with God. And as the apostles asked Jesus, "When will all these things happen?" Also Daniel asked the man clad in white linen who was above the waters, "How long shall it be till the end of these wonders?" And the man told him it would be for a time, two times, and half time; and that when the shattering of the power of the holy people comes to an end all these things would be accomplished.

"O my lord," cried Daniel in anguish to know more, "What shall be the issue of these things?"

"Go your way, Daniel," answered the man of unearthly appearance. "The words are shut up and sealed until the time of the end. Many shall purify themselves and make themselves white; but the wicked shall do wickedly; and none of the wicked shall understand. But you go your way till the end; and you shall rest and shall stand in your alloted place at the end of the days."

44. The Return to Judea
(536 B. C.)

The sufferings of captivity in Babylon together with the urgings and pleas of the prophets, especially Ezekiel and Daniel, had not only united Jews, but also awakened in them strong feelings of belonging to their faith. Daniel made a great impression not only on his fellow Jews, but also on Persians, starting with their kings and down the line. After Darius, whom Daniel converted to believe in and to serve the one true God, to the throne came king Cyrus. Being a spiritual seeker he was deeply impressed with the "new" Hebrew religion. He was one whom the prophet Isaiah long before had called "the Lord's anointed."

King Cyrus was a broad-minded and considerate emperor. His domain and power were great. Being tolerant he gave religious freedom to everyone in his kingdom, knowing that this was the chief factor in human happiness.

After conquering Babylon and learning the sad fate of the Jews, Cyrus, by divine inspiration, issued a proclamation that all Jews in his kingdom should go back to Jerusalem and rebuild the Temple of the Lord.

To prove that he really meant it, he restored to them the sacred vessels which Nebuchodonosor had carried away: 5400 vessels of gold and silver that belonged to the Temple. More than forty thousand Israelites under the leadership of Prince Zerubbabel and the High Priest Jeshua marched back to Judea. Peoples voices mixed with two hundred men and women singing in great jubilation the psalms of David on the way to their beloved Mother, Jerusalem.

Once they arrived in Jerusalem their spirits failed them. The once golden Jerusalem was nothing but a heap of ruins. No one was welcoming them. People who made their meager survival in the holy city were even resentful of the newcomers.

The returned remnants of the twelve tribes immediately built an altar on the spot where the Holy of Holies used to stand and offered sacrifice every morning and evening. A year later the foundations of the new Temple were laid. People rejoiced with trumpets and thanksgiving. And when after many years the Temple was completed, it was consecrated with great solemnity. Many of the old people remembering the former Temple wept because the new one did not equal the first one in mangnificence.

At the time of rebuilding the Temple the prophet Aggeus was one who gave encouragement and spiritual strength to his people. He warned the old men who had seen Solomon's Temple not to be sad, because the new one would be even more glorious than the first one: the Messiah would honor it with his presence.

> *"Yet one little while and I will move the heaven and the earth and the sea and the dry land. And I will move the nations and the Desired of the nations shall come and I will fill this house with glory, said the Lord of hosts. . . Great shall be the glory of this last house more than of the first."*

A similar prediction was made to prophet Zechariah:

> *"Rejoice greatly, O daughter of Sion, shout for joy, O daughter of Jerusalem. Behold thy king will come to thee, the just and Savior, he is poor and riding on an ass. . ."*

He foresaw that the Messiah would be sold for the price of a slave:

> *"And they weighed for my hire thirty pieces of silver."*

About eighty years after their return from captivity the Jews, by the command of the king of Persia, commenced to rebuild the walls of Jerusalem. Samaritans offered their help but were rejected by the Jews. This angered them. They opposed and tried to prevent the people from rebuilding the city. But the Jews prayed to God to assist them and God helped them.

The last of the Hebrew prophets (circa 450 B.C.) was Malachi. His prophecies, resembling those of Isaiah, give clear idea and promise to the coming Messiah.

> *"Behold, I send my messenger to prepare the way before me, and the Lord whom you seek will suddenly come to his temple; the messenger of the covenant in whom you delight, behold he is coming, says the Lord of hosts."*

As Isaiah was saying, "The voice of one crying in the desert: Prepare ye the way of the Lord, make straight in the wilderness the paths of God," so Malachi came even closer in his prophecy, "Behold, I will send Elias the prophet before the coming of the great and dreadful day of the Lord."

It seems that two comings of the Lord are predicted, the first coming of Christ and the second one on the Day of Judgment.

Malachi who tells us that a universal sacrifice, a clean oblation will supersede the offering of burnt animals in which the Lord God did not take pleasure anymore:

> *"I have no pleasure in you, says the Lord of hosts,*
> *and I will not accept an offering from your hand.*
> *For from the rising of the sun to its setting my*
> *name is great among the nations, and in every*
> *place incense is offered to my name, and a pure*
> *offering; for my name is great among the nations,*
> *says the Lord of hosts."*

This prophecy came true after the Last Supper — since then the sacrifices are offered from dawn to dawn all around the world by priests according to the order of Melchisedek, who was the forerunner of Christ sacrificing the clean oblation of bread and wine on the altar.

The dream of revelation of the promised Messiah came true four hundred years later. At that time Hebrews were torn and weakened by continual dissension among themselves. Not being able to settle their quarrels, they called upon the Romans to decide for them. The Romans settled the dispute by taking possession of Judea and placing on its throne Herod, a stranger and a collaborator with Caesar. Thus came the prophecy of Jacob to accomplishment: "The scepter shall not be taken away from Juda, till HE come that is to be sent, and HE shall be the expectation of nations."

Herod reigned in Judea when the Messiah so long promised and longed for, came on earth in human form, born in Bethlehem from the stock of Juda.

"Shower, O heavens, from above," cried once Isaiah, "And let the skies rain down the just; let the earth open, and bud forth the Savior."

MIDDLE EAST
2000 to 1000 B.C.

------ The Kingdom of David

0   100   200   300   400   500 km

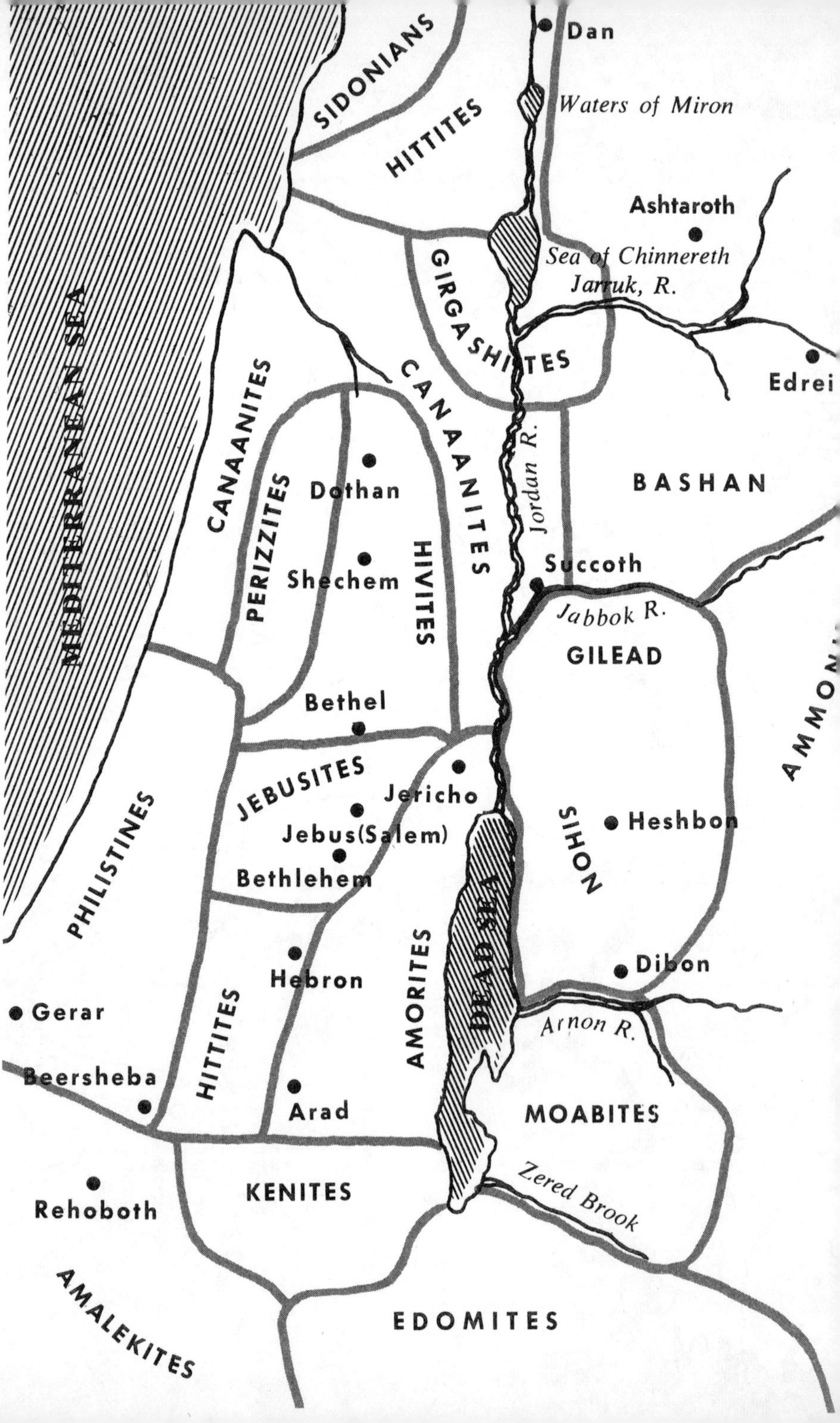

SIDONIANS
Dan
Waters of Miron
HITTITES
Ashtaroth
Sea of Chinnereth
Jarruk, R.
GIRGASHITES
MEDITERRANEAN SEA
Edrei
CANAANITES
CANAANITES
Jordan R.
BASHAN
PERIZZITES
Dothan
Shechem
HIVITES
Succoth
Jabbok R.
GILEAD
Bethel
JEBUSITES
Jericho
Jebus(Salem)
Bethlehem
PHILISTINES
SIHON
Heshbon
DEAD SEA
Hebron
AMORITES
Dibon
Gerar
HITTITES
Arnon R.
Beersheba
Arad
MOABITES
Zered Brook
Rehoboth
KENITES
AMALEKITES
EDOMITES